In The Days of Love

Durlabh Singh

chipmunkapublishing
the mental health publisher

Durlabh Singh

Published by
Chipmunkapublishing
PO Box 6872
Brentwood
Essex CM13 1ZT
United Kingdom

http://www.chipmunkapublishing.com

Copyright © Durlabh Singh 2010

Chipmunkapublishing gratefully acknowledge the support of Arts Council England.

Author Biography

Durlabh Singh is a writer and an artist based in London, England.

He has been published widely in over 300 publications worldwide.

His other publications include:
Chrome Red - Collected Poems.
Spaces of Heart - Illustrated Verse.
Kama Sutra of Love - Collections of Short Stories
Keeper of Reflections & Other Stories.
In The Days of Love - Novel.

Throughout his life, he had to struggle against the odds. Having lost his father at very early age, he had to take up the role of head of family, being the only male member in the household. Facing all the injustices of Indian social class system where he had to provide big dowries for marrying his sisters and getting into debts.

The things took turn for worse when he came to England, as extreme racism was rampant there when he was constantly ridiculed and set upon by gangs of youths. Landlords refused to rent him even a room and shopkeepers refused to serve. He was subject to racial taunts in streets and at work. He suffered number of physical attacks and partially lost sight of an eye as he was beaten in a busy London street. That constant harassment eventually resulted in acute depression and a mental breakdown and as a result he was admitted to a mental hospital.

He took up painting and writing as a therapy and developed these arts where he could find easier to breath from constant atmosphere of suffocation. It helped him to survive and keep his mental balance, in finding transcendence and wider fields of human creativity. People suffering from mental distress may find some solace in his works.

Chapter One

Smiling eyebrows are opened
Who does not know?
Yet nobody knows.

It can aptly be said about love. There are few of us who know about love and even fewer who practice this art of loving. No one can generalize about it; it is sufficient into itself and as such could be different for each individual.

The flat lands of Punjab have seen numerous kingdoms-tribes, people, poets and lovers.
It is an ancient land but has renewed itself so often, through its peoples and their movements that it seems to be always modern in all its aspects of culture and outlook.

On the typographical map, Punjab is marked at the head of Indian subcontinent and is situated at its northern most corners just below the Himalya mountain ranges with their perpetual snow. Its original Sanskrit name was designated by people in accordance with its perpetual icy bound crags. 'Him' means ice and 'alya' means the house, so the whole designation was given- Himalya as the house of snow or the house of ice. It took millions of years for Indian sub-continent to drift northwards from the south- pole and then as it collided with the Asian continent, the result was the formation of the high mountain chains, the highest mountain range in the world. It is still growing as the impact and pressure of Indian subcontinent plate keeps pushing itself against the Asian plate.

In summer seasons when the ice melted, a drainage system of rivers was established and the five rivers flowing through Punjab plains gave its name to the land as the 'land of five rivers' and thus the name came into existence.

It has these rivers running through its body, like the veins carrying its precious lifeblood. These life-giving waters have their resource in the lofty Himalya, in the land of icy Tibetan uplands, a plateau where various goddesses of the wilds have their abodes amid the high stony crags and the wild winds.

This land has seen the dawn of human history, spanning of various cultures. Once the poets and metaphysicians held their breath at the site of its fertile and lush plains, surrounded by the lofty mountains. They sang their praises of gratitude to its panoramic life – its birds, wildlife, warmth of its plains and its abundant harvests of grain and fruits. India is surrounded by lofty mountains in the north and the sea on its triangular shores and for the invaders to filter through, the only safe route had been, through some high passes across mountains in the northwestern frontier region the continent and through which the invaders had poured down at regular intervals into Punjab plains since the dawn of the history.

In common all the invaders wanted to capture the throne of Hindustan at Delhi, the heart of India but before they got to Delhi, they had to travel through Punjab and as a result this land bore the brunt of invading armies, with their pre-occupations for murders, rapes and loots. As a result the Punjabis have developed a fierce characteristics of fighting spirit, a taste for liberty and resistance.

Rang Mala was a pleasant village on the banks of the river Sutlej. It was not an enormous village but with a population of nearly two thousand souls it could hold its own. The land around the village was fertile due to network of irrigation canals and proximity of the river and this had led to prosperity of its people, both financially and culturally.

The head of Mahal family was a proud man and was the chief landowner of the village. He was the head of the local village council too and ran various charitable institutes. As a highly respected member of the community, all the village folks looked up to him. People sought his help and guidance whenever difficulties arose. He has a large family with four sons and two daughters.

Most of the sons and daughters were cunning, worldly-wise, and practical. Three sons were clever with their hands and brains, expert in tilling the land and managing their farms. They had been educated and their aim was to extend their family fortunes and bring greater prosperity by way of commerce, by branching out into other commercial enterprises.

The youngest son Karan Mahal was the exception to the rule and had been different from others since his birth, his father also noticed it. Karan always had that dreamy look about him and with his long hair and love of music; he had become unpopular with his brothers due to his 'feminine' ways. On the contrary he had become the favourite son of his father and that too, to the annoyance of his other brothers.

It seemed that his childhood was idyllic and often he felt like living in a kingdom of his own-some remote and romantic land full of kind folks and with fabulous beasts that roamed about freely in that land and not imprisoned in the little cages of the zoo. He had no sense of time as happened in most of the childhood. He felt safe and secure in that heavenly kingdom ruled by his father where everyone was of some privileged position.
Without any conception of time, he was living in a timeless universe and which to his infant mind, was going to last forever.

He went on long walks with his father, into deep countryside and for those moments he was most sensitive to the enchanting beauties of landscapes around him. The tall trees gave their shades of exquisite freshness and where he would sit down and contemplate about the natural beauty of his world. Once after following a narrow marked track used often by goatherds, he found himself on top of a mound and looked down on his village, which seemed to him bathed in celestial beauty of daylight. His father pointed out that the mound might have a buried treasure buried within it or possibly even a buried village of past and if an archeologist was to dig it, he was sure to find some pieces of pottery at least another paraphernalia hidden in the dust. His father further explained that through the history of that land there had been so many great civilizations, which were mighty in their own days but now lay under the ruins of dust forgotten.

Once it was springtime and the fields were golden with the advent of the mustard crop and its flowers. He wanted to see how far they stretched and for which he needed a vantage point. He slowly climbed the mound and looked around and the view was stunning. The yellow mustard fields stretched for miles and the colour was intoxicating to his senses and these become full and over brimmed. It was such an enchanting site and a miracle of nature and perhaps of the maker, creative genius behind it. Perhaps his little heart had touched the divinity. He was so thankful.

That made him to ponder and he thought that one day he might be able to fathom the past history of his land. He was pleased that so many new avenues were opening in his mind and for which he was grateful to his father. His father was impressed with the sensitivity of his youngest child and thus he became his favourite and to the annoyance of his brothers and sisters. They thought of him as a spoiled child and became jealous of as receiving the lion's a share of their father's love. His father pointed out that the child was sensitive to present and past history of the land and to which none would give any attention. They were insensitive to the field of archeology and to so many finer things of life.

In The Days of Love

Karan had his flute with him all the time and composed songs and music whenever he could. As in most of the families as an artistic talent, he was not appreciated and had bred contempt of other siblings. But to him the music was his need to exist, to take part in the whole panorama of life and moreover it had less material aspirations than the material outlook of his family and majority of mankind who were intent on making money at all cost; even at the expense of their emotional lives.

His solitude taught him wisdom and his music gave him an entrance into the reality of things both visible and invisible. He was amazed at relentless pulse of life but found that music gave him a static harmony in which his life could find a niche to stop for a moment. Most people considered that as an escape but to a sensitive mind like his, it was not an escape from life but a way in to a taste of life more intense. Real living took place at each instant and that instant was constantly moving and changing. The wise thing was to open one's heart to each moment and listen to the music in all its rawness before one's thinking turned it into an abstract pattern, conforming to pre- established conditioned modes and into which everybody was doing their utmost to escape to, under the dictates of biological complexes and conditionings.

His brothers hated his appearance, his mannerism, his dress code and his tenderness and sensitivity in dealing with others. It seemed that he would have a hard life ahead of him. The siblings considered him to be a slur on family's good name and that he was surely going to bring shame on his family.

All the brothers usually ganged up against him or against his idleness and despite his father's protest he was assigned to menial jobs like grazing the family's cattle in the fields. His brothers were overjoyed to find him in such a position as grazing the animals was considered to be the lowest menial job and was normally assigned to the outcasts of the society or to the lower classes of untouchables.

Without much protest Karan took this job and willingly took the cattle to the wilderness for grazing, on daily basis. He even began to like it as a great relief, away from family's constant bickering. Open fields, grasslands and wilderness suited his poetical temperament. He could respond emotionally to various seasons, different crops and changing lengths of the days and all the seasonal variations. He found inner peace and a harmony in the working of his flute in the music he played, in the songs he composed. Even cows, buffaloes, goats became his fans and listened to him attentively. People remarked that since he took up grazing, the cattle had become more docile and placid.

In the morning, Karan would unchain all the animals-buffaloes, cows and goats and with a lathi on his shoulder, he would direct the animals to the open fields outside the village boundaries. He was always on the lookouts for the fields of semi barren lands on which no crop could be cultivated but had plenty of fresh grass in their folds. He also looked for some trees with good foliage as to give protection from the afternoon sun when it became too hot to bear the sun more than a few moments. Here he felt the earth's current with its upward energy flew from sunrise to midday and then one's heart bore messages of hope and contentment. He became so enthusiastic about the warm rays of sun, which infused life and energy into his existence. After the night's cold embrace the little creatures and birds on the land extended their wings upwards to receive supplicants of the sun.

 It always prompted him to play on his flute some ascending notes, inspiring ones with grace in their feet and courage in their arms, to face the life with all its luminosities and shadows. It was different at mid- day when he had taken his meals and appeased his hunger and when he felt a daze coming over, to sleep away that laziness under the shades of the trees. To him it was an idealized existence with love of his father inside the home and love of countryside outdoors. He soon realized that there were riches and puzzles right before his mind's eye and one had to learn how to decipher those. All around him were forms and feelings, which were sort of symbols and if one could learn to decipher those, one could enter into new worlds of rich complexity and explorations. There were worlds within worlds and it was the task of his human brain not to get frightened of those but to find hidden truths behind these and which could make life tolerable and richer.

We were so conditioned by the obvious and mundane and found it hard to believe that there was something beyond the forms that are seen by our eyes us and ignored the realties behind these like the bees which were only interested in just extracting the juices from flowers in order to make honey, for its community at large and for the bee queen or its off springs. There were more things more meaningful beyond those utilitarian preoccupations. While living in that 'idealized' state of affairs, he had his secret fears too that it might end someday suddenly.

On day while working in the fields, Karan's father fainted and fell down. A labourer picked him up and brought him home. When the news went out, all the family came rushing in and gathered around his bed-worried, grim faced but trying to assure the father that he should not worry unduly as he was going to recover and get up soon to resume his normal duties but he knew it instinctively that there was something drastically wrong within his body.

Nobody bothered to tell Karan about the bad news and only when he arrived home in the evening after grazing the cattle that he was told about it. He straightaway ran to his father's bedside and crying put his head on his father's chest. His father caressed and kissed him and told him that he was going to be well soon and would be with him for many moons to come.

But as the days passed his father began to wither away slowly under the onslaught of some deadly disease. As the time passed the family became used to the situation and did not much bothered about him and left him alone to cope with his illness on his own. Karan was the only one to look after him and cared tenderly for his father, forgetting his sleep and work, to the annoyance of his brothers, as they have to employ someone else for grazing the animals.

His father was getting weaker and weaker and with it a loss of body weight. Each day he had to be carried in his arms by Karan for bathing and other bodily functions. He ate less and less and when Karan carried him around, the father became like a bag of bones with haggard face and grisly form and that caused much grief to the compassionate heart of Karan. After about six months of illness, the physician told the family that there was not much hope left for him and that in a few days time he would leave his mortal remains behind. Karan's mind became agitated and as a consequence of his inability to share his grief with others a great depression ascended on him.

The day his father died he collapsed with grief and was much abused by his brother for such 'womanly' behaviour, resulting in great amount of shrieks and lamentation. It was first time that he had seen a dying person and had to come face to face with death in all its grisly tragedy. It was strange to see a person lying there as a corpse with no human face to communicate with. How could a person to whom you have loved all your life disappears in an instant and never to return again and never to receive any warmth and love from him anymore? What was the use of having all those relationship and attachments and which could end like that suddenly?

In The Days of Love

At last funeral rites were observed and he saw the funeral pyre on which his father's body was burning. The tongues of flame licked it; with hungry hissing and crackling noises until it was turned into a black mass of charred bones and which in the end became a heap of ashes. His mind became numb looking at it and he lost his sense of living and any taste for life at that moment.

After forty days of mourning his family gathered to talk about the things and directions to which the family was going to go. They had to divide the land, property and the money left behind by the deceased. The shares due to the girls were set aside for their dowries as to when the girls got married. They did not think that Karan deserved equal share of that booty and was deemed as not deserving anything out of their father's estate. When he protested he was just assigned a barren piece of land where he could graze the family's cattle. The best arable land and finest property went to his brothers.

Suddenly without his father, he had become a stranger to the family as everybody ignored him and he was left on his own even to cook his own meals. Once when he tried to stand for himself against the will of the family and confronted them, he only suffered abuse and physical violence. He found his own home turned into a prison with hostility and suffocation around him. Why to cling to those things, which no longer belonged to you? He decided to leave his village for good.

The day of departure for Karan soon arrived. At night he went into his room and gathered all his belongings, which did not amount to much and tied them into a bundle to carry over his shoulders through the journey .In the morning while it was still dark, he stepped out of the house into the open road under the cloudless skies. It was early and still dark and that was to avoid the prying eyes of his neighbours and curious villagers .The skies were full with countless stars hanging around in silent whispers. Lots of them were twinkling as if beckoning to Karan. He thought that those clusters of the stars were like the lighted lamps of a Diwali night's illuminations.

He wondered whether there were other worlds like his own and inhabited by folks like him, perhaps suffering pain and degradations and going outdoors in their nights to seek some solace from the universe at large. He wanted to get lost in that array of brilliant diamonds. The fields, irrigation canals and even the air seemed to reflect their glory. For a moment he forgot his loneliness and sat on a boulder in contemplation, praising such miracles of nature.

He woke up from the reverie by barking of a lone dog, heralding the arrival of the dawn and soon other dogs responded indicating that they were awake too and a symphony of barking ensued. A farmer scolded the dog for waking him up so early, with few hours of comfort left to taste the warmth of his bed.

After leaving his village and for want of direction, he just followed the river and walked along its mounded banks. The ground was wet with dewy grass and small birds were fluttering in and out of the tall reeds along the bank. In the dim light the river looked like a molten line of glistening waters. Soon the orange disc of the sun would appear and dye the landscape in its golden colour. The coolness of the air would disappear; bring in first the warmth and then the oppressive heat of the day would ensue. It was a good time to travel.

*

His heart was a bit lighter but soon the remembrance of things past returned and turned into a heavy burden. He again remembered the death of his father and things turned sour in his mind. When a person who was close to you suddenly vanishes, that leaves a terrible vacuum behind. When they are alive and with you, you take them for granted and even never realize that they had carved a niche within yourself and which unknowingly becomes a part of your life. You were glad to carry that human warmth around you giving a meaning and purpose to life but when those are removed by a stroke of bad luck, it became so hard to recover from that cruel blow. It would take time in getting used to it.

You try to lock that quarters of being, which used to be their place of residence and then forgot about it for a while but then the guilt those memories still residing memory there and found that anguish restored and thus you suffered doubly.

It was getting lighter now. The sun had sent its scouts to clear the ways for its arrival. Soon that proclamation spread around and a flock of birds took to sky, to greet the arrival of the sun. They flew in unison formation with exquisite mass movements engendered by some inner drives and that kept going in a dance formation for some time.

Few farmers were all ready up and moving to their fields. The set their wooden ploughs on their shoulders with their bullocks leading the way. They were clicking their tongues to direct the broad shouldered oxen. The oxen were making pleasing movements with their head bobbing, setting in motion the jingling music of tiny bells, worn around their necks.
Soon they passed and gradually the music faded away in the clear light of the day.

*

He had been walking for few hours and was feeling tired and decided to rest by the edge of the water. He saw his own reflection in the water in broken rippled fragments but then more clearly. He noticed that the reflection was looking at him and beckoned him to come closer and greet him.

He walked into the shallow waters and the reflection conveyed that there was a way out of his anguish and he should come to meet it in the depths of the river where he would encounter the easeful death and end of his being. He fell into a trance and his thinking faculty was turned off momentarily. He decided to jump into the river.

A Sheppard walked into the vicinity with his flock of goats and suddenly the reality shock brought Karan to his senses and he woke with a sudden start. He saw a distant temple spiral and followed the path towards it and soon he was in the temple compound. He was hungry and tired and put his bundle against the wall to support him and sat there contemplating the countryside and his own fate.

He soon fell asleep escaping the painful thoughts into a sort of semi oblivion state but soon was awakened by a human noise and saw himself surrounded by an army of lay abouts. There were as usual the village simpletons- work-shy beggars and other lazy lads who wanted to escape the hard task of tilling the ground and from farm work on their fathers' land.

They were staring at him, waiting for him to wake up and had stolen his flute and on which they were trying to play a tune to the amusement of the gathered crowd. Each one was trying in his turn but a pitiful jarring noise was coming at the other end of the flute. It did not bother the crowd and they were clapping, dancing, shrieking and laughing at the antics of the bad players. When they saw Karan waking up, they urged him to play something on his flute to cheer them.

In The Days of Love

Karan was surprised at their demands as he did not know them and neither they knew about his flute playing. It seems that his reputation had already preceded his arrival.
He was in no mood to entertain the crowd and this annoyed the crowd a great deal.

Two lads came around and started chatting to him. Karan could not detect whether they were simpletons or were just clever enough to exploit him emotionally to gain their ends. They did not seem to him bearing any malice towards him but simply were trying to goad him to play some music on his flute. When he refused they flattered him with all sort of niceties. They told him they he was great musician who stole people's heart with the depth of his music. Soon they brought a donkey and offered to give him a ride on that stallion. Karan looked at the half starved donkey with its meek and humble looks and felt a sort of kinship with it and that softened his heart.

Some farmer's wives passed by carrying food for their husbands in the fields as their midday meal. They were carrying pots of sour milk on their heads and bundles of chapattis and saag wrapped around cleanly and tucked in their scarves. The sight of the crowd tickled their curiosity and they came around to look as to what was happening. It was pleasant to break their routine of monotony and talk to someone belonging to a different village.

When they saw Karan sitting there haggard and tired looking, they offered him some food in exchange for some music, to be played on his flute. These were gentle women and good-looking too and soon their charms did the trick and he offered to play something for them in exchange for morsels of their food. They put some chapattis and cooked vegetables on a plate and gave him and then poured some sour milk for drink. He had been so engrossed in his grief and had not spoken to anybody for some time and it was pleasant to eat their tasty food and get into music and pleasant and conversation.

He took the flute, put to his lips and blew into it and involuntary a passionate tune came forth at the other end. Receding and advancing telling tales of some sorrow and tears about the life's vagaries and injustices, of loneliness of each being and a search for a little love. It touched every heart in that congregation and some even had a lump in their throats. The sound of s music brought in a bigger crowd and even shepherds with their flock came to listen. Karans soon forget his loneliness and tunes just poured in. The magic of the music induced in everyone a sort of sympathy for each other and a human companionship.

The playing went on for some time until the farmers wives decided to leave as their husbands were waiting for the mid day meal and any delay was bound to cause some friction and suspicion in their minds. Karan was glad to have met those pretty ladies and having eaten their food but the gatherings of layabouts was not so easy to cope with. They have caught a mood of enjoyment for themselves which did not happen often in their lives and so were ready to prolong that period irrespective of whether they were annoying him or not. They pulled Karan within a human circle and urged him to play more and more but he refused. They appealed to his finer emotions to take pity on them as their lives were full of misery and the least thing he could do was to give them more music for some relief and let them indulge in a bit of entertainment. There was nothing to stop them now as they were dancing, shrieking or just jumping about.

As the afternoon rolled on and the shadows lengthened, the mob slowly moved away and Karan's anxiety returned in with a double dose. Where he was going to go, what was he going to do with his life? He thought about his next move and that was hard to envisage. As happened in those moments of indecisions, he decided to stay put at the temple for at least that night to think it over.

Soon the priest of the temple came along to open it for the evening prayers but was not pleased to see him there. He unlocked the inner sanctuary but told him to stay out and not to enter that holy sanctuary. Karan was hurt by this treatment and was annoyed with the priest and straight away asked him the reason for it. The priest told him that he could see that there were no good qualities in him, he was a vagabond without any hearth or home and furthermore he was corrupting the youths with his music and thus leading them into bad ways vagrancy and lewdness.

Karan told him that he did not have much respect for his kind of priesthood too, he was misleading the people too with his outward masquerade of piety but inside he was cunning like a fox. He had found a good way of deceiving people by granting them the divine protection of religion in exchange for few pieces of silver. Lots of barren women were coming to his sanctuary and he was performing rituals for their fertility and giving them sacred threads and amulets to be worn around their necks. Furthermore he was not even sure whether he was taking some advantage of those poor women behind their husband's backs. That annoyed the priest.

There were more heated arguments between the two and at one time the enraged priest had the intention of taking Karan by the lapel and physically throw him out of the temple but was put off by the arrival of some evening worshippers. The priest thought it was best to keep quiet in front of his congregation. He told Karan that he could spend the night in the temple complex but had to move away before the dawn of the following day, to make his own way.

The priest came to the temple very early in the morning while Karan was still asleep and shook him violently and told him to get up, which woke him with a sudden start He did not know what was happening as he was still dazed with the sleep. The priest told him to roll up his bedding, collect his things and be out of his temple immediately. Karan told him to let him sleep a little more until the sunrise but he would not listen to any pleadings. Karan gathered up all his possessions and as soon he was out of the temple door the priest locked the doors behind him and without any further ado went away on his way to some other business.

Stupefied and half dazed, Karan sat on the temple steps till it was sunrise. He had suffered enough humiliations from each one and sundry and was really hurt by all that mistreatment. He had no plan as what to do next and he decided to walk again by the river in the direction he had already taken. He conjectured that there must be other human habitations and possibly a village somewhere, where he would try to find some work and a roof. He was not afraid of any hard work and was not particular bothered any with any sort of work as long as he was treated with a little respect. He could just keep his body and soul together.

Soon the morning arrived and sun was up, he was just starting his journey and he saw some figures coming towards him and when they came near him he recognized two of the lads from previous night's fracas. They were with a donkey and seemed to be as happy as larks. They introduced themselves as the two village boys, Ramu and Shamu. Karan recognized them as the village simpletons from the previous episode and did not want to get involved with them.

'Where are you going?' Ramu asked him

'I do not know.' Karan replied trying to put them off.

Both were in grips of laughter and were so pleased with his answer.

'That is the best way to travel when you do not know where you are going' they replied,
and agreed with each other that the best way to travel was one when one was not aware of one's direction or destiny. When you did not know a single thing that meant you know everything. That was the logic the two simpletons were indulging in. Karan thought they were trying to make a fool of him but when he looked in their faces there was no trace of either malice or ridicule, they generally believed in what they were saying and furthermore he thought they were trying to help him.

They asked him whether he had his breakfast and when Karan replied that he had not and also he could not afford it as he had no money on him, their faces dropped as if there was a genuine concerned about him. They told him that they were going to do something about it. Ramu found some old bricks in the fields and with these he made a sort of fireplace while Shammu went in search for some dry branches and discarded twigs. From a satchel astride the donkey's back, they took out a metallic vessel to boil the water. While the water was boiling, they brought out some cups and some stale rotis. They made some tea and invited Karan to take his breakfast. Although he found it ridiculous, he was touched. The fools showed a genuine concern for a weary traveler.

After finishing the breakfast, the simpletons became more animated and started praising Karan.

'We like you.'
'We love you'
'You are great'
You are a great musician'
'You inspire us with your dreams.'

All theses compliments had adverse effect on Karan: he knew that he was not great and he was without a home and without any means of earning a living, he had never studied with a master and all that he learnt was with his own effort as a self taught flute player. When he told these to the simpletons they told him that they did not care about any of those things and the important thing was that his music moved them and that they were capable of appreciating any good music when they heard one. Karan was surprised at that as whom he thought as ignorant layabouts had a spark of intelligence and he felt more sympathetic towards them

Soon they wanted to learn flute playing from him but when he told them that it took him years to perfect that art; they simply ignored him and still wanted to learn. He tried to make another excuse that he had no spare flutes with him to teach them on with but they simply pulled out flutes from their bag, Karan was stuck with them without any more excuses. Three of them sat on the grassy bank beside the river and it was nice setting with the waters of the river slowly meandering and the morning sunshine warming the landscape around them and the poor donkey standing and basking in it.

Inspired by his surroundings, he composed a spontaneous tune and told them to copy and play that tune on their respective flutes. Jarring annoying noises came from their flutes. Karin taught them as how to hold the flute in their hands in a proper manner and how to blow through it with one's lips and slowly the simpletons got the hang and began to imitate him note by note. They were simply delighted with their efforts and started dancing while playing rudimentary tunes on their flutes.

After that taxing session the simpletons were exhausted and wanted to take some rest. They lay down on the grass verge and rolled themselves to and fro and thus recovered their usual exuberant behaviour. In spite of his protests they put him on their donkey and wanted to accompany him on his journey onwards. He was riding the donkey and the two simpletons were playing their flutes and singing beside him. It was quite a spectacle and brought smiles on the passing onlookers' faces. After a few miles the simpletons had enough of dancing and music making and left him. He carried on his journey hoping to hit another village soon.

Chapter Two

The Lalit family lived in a large village few miles from the river and the head of the family Nihal lalit owned a large track of land, which he used wisely to plant a variety of crops. The farm was always busy with people planting, cultivating and tilling the land for wheat, maize, sugar canes, fruits and vegetables. He lived in a big house with his wife Lachi and his two offspring, a boy and a girl .His son's name was Mohan and who was the first-born. He was fairly satisfied with his life but still was a great worrier especially when he had to confront things, which he had not experienced before. He was of polite nature and tended to treat everyone with respect. When anyone spoke to him harshly or with malice resulting in verbal abuse, he went into a tailspin and into an introspect examination of himself as to see whether it was his fault to incur other's roth. Though he came of farming stock, his outlook on life was not confined to farming only. He had acquired some broader aspects of living. He was captivated by the nature and its miracle and was always on look out for something deeper in his life.

When he looked around him and on the countryside, he was fascinated by the exuberance of natural processes. The blue skies, the clouds playing there transforming themselves into a variety of shapes and sizes. The rich brown earth, the azure skies and the fleecy white - these were the painted scenes that induced in him a sort of trance and brought to him some complex feelings into which his normal logical mind could never dared to venture.

He found that there were so many things for which his daily routine had no inclination to probe into. Most men were cut off from greater realities of the existence. Everybody was simply occupied with their own concerns as a part of human race or its survival, resulting in the welfare of their respective families. Being born, growing up, marrying, producing children and then dying- was it all? Surely this grand universe must have secrets locked away somewhere, hidden from the eyes of the mankind somewhere beyond the trivial pursuits of mankind.

Though of delicate mind and constitution he wanted to probe into those tedious questions, whenever he could even at the expense of putting constrains on his delicate mind. Where do we come from and where do we go from here? like everybody else, he was preoccupied with such question. Words of great teachers or of religious holy men were not sufficient for him to reconcile with his own inner feelings. As in order to quench one's hunger, one had to eat oneself and this hunger would not be appeased just by looking at other men eating their own foods, in a manner of speaking. These were the questions constantly arising in his mind but he could not share these with anyone else for fear of being ridiculed.

His wife's health had been fragile and when she became pregnant the second time, this was the cause of a great deal worry to Nihal. In order to show his love and concern, he bought scores of gifts for her. He prayed and prayed for his wife's good health and when she went into labour, it was just the undoing of him. The period of labour lasted nearly three days, during which he could not sleep or eat properly and sat there all the time in front of the door of delivery room, where his wife was going to give birth. He became a nervous wreck and perspired profusely in spite of so many people's assurances and consolations. He simply could not cope with all that pressure and thus was removed by force by the midwife to a place away from that location. He simply suffered periods of emotional hell.

All the time his ears were pinned towards that direction, of any sound coming from that room and when he heard the shrill cry of the child he rushed forward to see the midwife and the midwife assured him that all was well and both mother and child were doing fine. He was taken to the bedside and immediately hugged and kissed his wife. His wife was holding a small bundle in her arms with the newborn wrapped in it. She handed him the bundle and he tenderly took it, though with shaking hands and unwrapped it, he was overjoyed to see his daughter's face first time. She shone like a new moon after many a dark nights. He remarked that the child was the prettiest he had ever seen and named it Sohni or the beautiful one.

With the passing of the time the child grew and was intensely active and lively. She became full of physical vigour, endurance and above all in possession of all the graces to which a father could aspire to. The father was bowled over by all the small activities of the child and when she uttered her first word, he distributed to the poor plenty of alms. He was very proud and showed it through his constant talk about his daughter's charms to everybody he met. When she started constructing her first sentences, he liked those sweet nothings to some high poetry and told people all about her first uttering's and all this to the amusement of other folks.

Whenever he took her out into the streets, he was surrounded by the people who wanted to congratulate him on having such a sweet child and everybody either wanted to touch her or lift the child into their arms. He was so proud accompanied by that child so full of grace. Eventually he took her to his fields to show her the processes of cultivation, extent of his land and its working. Seeing other farmers labouring, she wanted to do likewise. She was fascinated by the ploughs tilling the ground and turning the soil upside down and she became fond of oxen too, dragging the ploughs behind them. Her father bought her small fabrics of different colours, which she made into cloth necklaces for the oxen, attaching lots of jingling bells.

In The Days of Love

She tied these around the necks of her favourite oxen and when they moved, there was a symphony of jingling music, to which she danced to and made merriment. She had all the exuberances of a lively child. She gladdened all the folk's heart and her spontaneous display of affection made her very popular with the whole village.

It may be observed that the children, who are born pretty and sweet as babies, do not always retain their qualities of temperament as they grow up into their teens or adulthood. It may be that the effects of being praised or being liked by everyone create a sort of cushioning effect against the harsh realities of life but who wants to suffer more by struggling on one self in every day's life? It is ok on one level but gain in one direction is always loss in other direction. You develop your character only by overcoming the obstacles in one's life and thus you grow and develop your qualities of character.

But it was otherwise with Sohni who retained her prettiness or even surpassed it with passing of years and yet remained a center of attraction for the people for her human qualities. Young men could not take their eyes off her beautiful form and face. Her eyes darted around wounding their hearts and even the old men became jealous of the young men admiring her beauty. Such was the magic of her charm, both of body and mind.

Sohni was like a new flower in bloom, a flower which did not have any sense of time, it did not know its past history or like a plant being born out of a seed kept buried in dark recesses of the earth from which it shot forth and shone forth in the full glory of dazzling sunshine and in the warmth of a balmy breeze. Its flower's being was concerned with its own glory and its task was to be involved in its blooming petals and in giving radiating life and being alive to its surroundings. All those who looked upon its glory and waned to indulge in that glory but with the older generation it came with a tinge of melancholy. A melancholy bred through the knowledge that even all that brightness was of brevity like the human life, which was always rushing towards the dark shadows of the death.

Sohni was such a rare flower who was only interested in its task of simply blooming without any care of past or future. Her youth had that innocence which like a playful kitten had no inkling about the hardness and sufferings of life to come. Being the daughter of a prosperous father, she had never known the lack of money or material wants. She thought that her kind of life would continue forever or at least for few years to come. Sometime she would hear some of her friend getting engaged and eventually getting married and then she thought about it but did not like the idea of the same pattern being repeated over and over again treaded by people on the oft repeated paths of their lives. If everybody was to follow the predetermined path in life there was not be any great achievements. One had to find an alternative path full of newness or some sort of creativity bringing in certain emotional adventure.

Not only she was of pretty countenance but combined within her strength of character too, which was a rare phenomenon. Her personality acquired a charismatic hue, which affected greatly all those who came into to her presence or talked to her face to face. She became fearless in her behaviour but full of fairness to all and sundry. Big landlords and men of influence had no sympathy or care for the poor or the lower strata of the society and thus she became a champion of such people.

Poor and neglected folks started coming to her for help or for any sensible advice. Though she helped some with financial help but it was not all the people were seeking from her. They wanted moral support or just a word of advice or a word of comfort to sooth their wounded selves and she was clever enough to supply these in abundance.

Whenever there was a dispute between the landlords and their workers she intervened and initially was not very popular with the big guns of the village but soon overcame such obstacles. Her force of personality and her determinedness slowly overcame the big landlords and other dignitary. Unconsciously her beauty was the winning charm, which they could not resist. In the end she acquired a reputation for her fair mindedness and justice.

 She became fond of any running waters whether it was a canal or the big river. Her father lead a busy life and had to go on frequent trips either to consult other farmers or to sell his produce in the market place and instead of horse and buggy he found it convenient to travel by a riverboat. At the insistence of her daughter he ordered a boat of his own to travel up and down the river and began to take her daughter with him often for companionship or for consultancy on matters of finance and dealing with difficult people.

She began to go on the water herself more frequently as she liked the feel of flowing waters. She added a small compartment to the boat as a shelter from rain and added in a nice couch in it to relax. She learnt the art of rowing from his father and other experts and soon was taking the boat on her own. She rowed the boat upstream and then let it go downstream. She relaxed on her couch, dreamily observing the reeds flowing past the river banks and when little birds fluttered out of their hiding places, she loved it so much. She quacked with the ducks in her own imitation and took food leftovers to feed the watery fowls.

 One morning Sohni got up early while still dark and waited for the sun to come up and soon the air was filled with songs of the bird with an occasional squawk of a peacock. The long stalks and the plants with their thick leaves did a gentle dance in the breeze. Some were still wet with the overnight frost and the sun melting their white coverings into shiny drops of golden liquid.

At the suggestion of her friends she was going to indulge in a day of make-ups for her body and face. Soon a bevy of friends arrived and holding each other in a circle they danced, giggled and enjoyed themselves in keeping with the glorious weather. Then that giggly group of girls surrounded her teasing her, prepared a tub of warm water for her bathing. They put rose petals into the water to perfume it and then prepared a paste of gram flour mixed with milk as an aid to freshen her skin. They applied that paste to her face and the body and rubbed it slowly into her skin until it was fairly dry and began to peel off and its nodules fell to the ground. They peeled off the rest of the dry mixture.

 She was bathed with the warm water and many delicate hands caressed her skin, washed it with herbal lotions until the skin was gleaming with freshness. She came out of the bath and was held gently into towels. She was put in front of a mirror for her makeup. Perfumed oil was messaged into her long hair and then a comb was applied to sort out the tangles. She was dressed into a green shirt and white trousers. They put some rouge on her cheeks made from sandal wood mixture and dyed her lips with the juice made from the bark of a special tree. Sohni put kajla into her eyes as a part of accentuating it and her eyes began to dart like shiny cobras spitting their charms onto the unsuspected victims.

When she looked into the mirror, her reflection defined a full-mooned face, silhouetted by dark clouds of her tresses. She blushed. It was a sight to behold,

'Sohni looks like a hoori from the paradise.' cried the friends.

In The Days of Love

' With that beauty you will murder all the lads of the village' they teased her.

' I am going to go into the village and warn all the folks that Sohni is arriving soon to kill
the people with her beauty and dangerous arrows of her glances.'

The troupe of the girls started moving all dressed in their finery and looking like a bunch of butterflies in a flowery garden. People looked and admired their beauty and their charms were overpowering. Older people looked on and sighed and were sorry for their lost youth and regretted its passing. They had been reminded of the things that pass and never to come again and this made them sad and also they were reminded of the shortness of their existence too. Soon they would be confronting the shadows in their demise.

The girls moved through the fields, through miles and miles of green vistas, of the growing crops and wherever they passed they attracted the attention of the men working in the fields. Attracted by their graceful figures, they became enamoured and stung by pangs of love. The beauty of a women worked both ways as a soothing balm to sooth disturbed hearts or as a fire to enflame them to bring out all their passions.

Soon they were on the riverside and found some lush grasses growing by its side. They put sheets over it and just poured themselves over. It was spring and mid day and they were feeling hungry. They have brought enough food for all those hungry souls, unpacked it and distributed the shares to each and began enjoying it. The pleasant weather and the amiable company made it doubly tasty and invigorating.

After having a splendid lunch, they spread themselves over the sheets and began to sing songs. Everybody contributed, they bold one first and the shy ones last, goaded by encouragement and bravos of the others. They got up then and began to dance, pair of girls joining- holding hands and pulling each other in a circle, a kikli dance of rigorous physical movement. There were girlish giggles and new games to play were devised and new stories to tell recounted and thus no go gossip was wasted.

*

Sohni's father was fond of music in his youth but when he married his interest waned. When his daughter showed interest in it, he revived his interest too in music again and one day he heard a musician plying an instrument at a friend's house, he found that classical music was soothing for his soul. There were roving minstrels covering the countryside and when they saw gatherings of villagers, they performed their singing accompanied by folk instruments, all to the entertainment of the village folks.

 Sometime these musicians played in the village squares where people gathered to listen. They sang songs usually composed by themselves. They sang about folk tales, old love lores, tales of sufferings, of wars and victims and of the heroes who fought for the liberation of their enslaved country by sacrificing themselves in the cause of liberty. Their profession consisted of composing songs and music for the masses on which they depended for their livelihood. People indulged in the music mainly for two reasons- for their entertainment or for the refinement of their tastes and souls. As these people were periodically trampled upon by the foreign invaders, they preferred the tales of heroes who put constant fights against the foreign oppressors.

Slowly her father extended his musical taste to classical mode as one day heard it being performed in a friend's house when he was bowled over with its intricacies- of shades of emotions it was expressing and decided to organize a concert of his own at his home and invited a sitar maestro to participate.

He used his spacious courtyard for this purpose and put up a dais for the sitarist and his accompaniments, to sit on the stage and to give the long recital. There were also the tabla and the tambura player to accompany the sitarist. He decked the stage with flowers, flags and multicolored pieces of fabrics to make it look splendid in a colorful visual display. He invited all the villagers to come and enjoy the concert free, which was something new for the village folks as they never had been to a concert before in their lives.

The sitar was fashioned out of seasoned gourd and the teakwood and had seven main playing strings above the board and numerious other sympathetic strings below. When the musician hand plucked the main strings, the sympathetic strings resonated in its promptings, pouring out array of harmony and tunes affecting the audiences' subtle mind. The watery steely notes arose and went straight to people's heart who were put into a sort of trance losing their identities and just fused into the music and thus becoming music themselves in all its tunes. They seem to have recovered their hidden souls and momentary forgot their day today problems and petty pre-occupations. It was as if the music had purified their inner self eliminating all the dross accumulated by trivialities of their living over along period of time. It was so freshening to feel again and experience the high drama.

The maestro started his recital with an alap or the slow un-accompanied movement to set the mood for the music, for audiences gathered around. There were people of all denominations, rich and poor, educated and illiterate, refined and not so refined .As soon as they tuned in to music they became hooked to it, even those who had never listened to the classical music before. They imagined being the maestro themselves and totally identified with the music and the musicians. As the maestro moved his hands along the strings on the board, their hands involuntary moved too imitating his movements.

Soon the tranquil notes of slow movement of alap gave way to faster jhor and the tabla started its accompaniment. Some vigorous tunes started their journeys as if an athlete had started racing on a long lap. Alap had prepared the audiences for a quite tranquil mood previously but now they had to move forward, jumping with energetic movements into a field of mental actions. The jhor was like some military steps or an army going forward, doubling into a trot. The responsive audiences gave shouts of bravo with such enthusiasm that the maestro was encouraged and began to explore different variations and themes in an improvised mode. The composition of the recital was not written down in any details, only just the notes were assigned to a particular raag and rest was to his improvisation and which was the normal thing to do on such occasions. No two recitals were identical and it showed a true mark of fresh creativity at each recital.

It was evening outside and the music imitated the moods of the saffron yellow light, the tumultuous disturbances of the clouds and it lead into an evening raag, just slowly melting into the darkening skies. The audiences sought the contents of the music with their expanded faculties. In reality it was only teakwood board studded with steel strings but what a non-material out pourings was issuing forth from that instrument. It was that reality essence which was affecting the audiences and their feelings. How long would they retain that heightened emotional state? Nobody knew. The recital came to an end and then at last the audiences broke and dispersed to their homes. They thought highly of the concert and considered it worthwhile for coming and listening. It taught them a great deal about the music and different musical instruments, which some had seen it their first time in their lives.

In The Days of Love

*

In ancient India a human being was not considered a complete person unless he/she had developed all the faculties of human mind- sixteen in number pertaining to arts, sciences, beauty, morality, ethics, metaphysics and so on. It seems Sohni was trying to acquire and develop as many as she could. When she heard the classical music on the sitar first time, it opened a new world to her and which she dearly wanted to preserve and even develop her potentials in other fields.

It is said that a human being acquired certain traits of character during their formative years of childhood and which in later life could still subsist in their psyche though in a hidden state. As we have seen earlier that when she was child, she developed a certain fondness for the animals and especially for the farm animal. She admired the hard work done by the oxen with their beauty and grace but she was annoyed to see the cruel treatment handed to these poor dumb creatures by their so called masters or the farmers. The animals were underfed, overworked and abused. They worked from dawn to dusk tilling the hard ground, carrying the yokes of the ploughs on their shoulders and when they got tired, they were not given any time for recuperations to restore their spent energies. Sometime they got stuck in tilling the hard ground or in muddy fields when they got whipped and physically mishandled. They were not free and had to perform a day-to-day routine, of hard physical labours like slaves.

That was not all. Once they had finished their task of operating the ploughs they were put onto the working for irrigation system and in operation of water wheel when they went round and round pulling the yoke of harness attached to levers of a wheel of a well, bringing a chain of pots full of water, dredged from the deep water reservoir. When they finished theses chores, they were further harnessed in pulling bullock carts whenever the farmers or their families traveled to the towns. It was a tough task and hard labour to perform

When the harvest was over, they pulled the carts loaded with grain intended for the market. After the grain extraction the remainder of the chaff left was removed to the storage as fodder for the animals during rest of the year. One could see that their lives were not happy. They had been castrated, starved, overworked and that was not the kind of life one could envisage for oneself. The cycle of their lives consisted in being yoked to hard work and then dying of exertions or of old age.

Often she complained about these things to the farmers but nobody was interested in improving their lot and everyone simply blamed that state on the poor animal's karma of the past lives. They must have committed bad deeds indeed in their previous lives and consequently they were just suffering the results of their previous misdeeds. It was all pre-destined by the gods and nobody could do anything about it. Sohni was simply shocked by those 'do nothing' attitudes. Her friends were very fond of her and respected her for her views of justice and concerns for downtrodden or poor and unjustly treated. This included not only humans but also all the animal kingdom.

She spoke passionately about her concerns and her love of animals and especially for those who assisted mankind in production of food for their survival. More and more people began to listen to her and began to assist her by reporting the people who was exploiting and abusing the farm animals. Someone reported that a rich farmer was mistreating his oxen.

Sohni and friends carried out a secret surveillance on the farmer and about his workings at this farm. They found a few malnourished creatures including an ox, very thin and its ribs showing through its wrinkled skin. It looked like half starved and just turning into a skeleton. There were wounds on its shoulder from which blood was oozing. It sprawled on the ground unable to lift itself from the ground unaided.

Soon the farmer came out, kicked and cursed the animal as a 'lazy bastard' and began to strike it with a stick. Sohni could not control herself and came out of her hiding and confronted the farmer.

'Shame on you, for beating the poor animal '

'Who are you to tread on my private land and speak to me in such a tone?'

'Stop beating the animal, you should be ashamed of yourself for such behaviour. '

' I can do what I like with my animal.' The farmer replied in defiance and raised his stick to inflict another blow to the animal.

Before the blow could fall on the ox, Sohni rushed forward and grabbed his hands to divert the blow onto a tree trunk where the animal lay crawled.

The farmer was furious and came to hit the Sohni but her friends rushed forward and pushed the farmer to the ground thus saving her.

The farmer felt humiliated being brought down by a troupe of young girls but lifted himself off the ground and after dusting off his clothes, he retorted

'You have attacked me and I am going to report it to the village council.'

'You go ahead and we will report also to the council that you are starving and inflicting cruelties on your farm animals.'

' But these are my animals and I own them and furthermore I can do anything on my farm and whip any lazy animal as to give me proper service.'

'No you cannot, someone has to stand for the dumb creatures.' The girls answered

' But all these animals are my property and I have the right to do anything... I have got the rights.'

' No one owns anything in this world. All are God's creatures.'

The farmer was strung with all that rubbish which he regarded as sentimentalism and a sort of cheap preaching and which he hated.

' You can see that the creature is bleeding and starved and you have been using it forcibly to do all the hard work. You can further see the marks of wooden plough which with persistent use had rubbed and peeled off its skin to the bone with blood is oozing. Soon it will be infected. If you keep treating the creature, the poor thing is going to die.'

The farmer realized that the girls were telling the truth but at a last resort and saving his face, he retorted:

' I am a poor farmer and I cannot afford to lay the land untilled, you are trying to make me starve without a single grain coming from the next harvest.'

Everybody laughed, as they knew that he was a rich farmer and could afford to buy more animals.

In The Days of Love

He looked at the girls and saw faces of the daughters of the prominent people belonging to the village and thought it was a good policy to agree with the girls in order to avoid any further trouble and so apologized to them, promising to follow better practices on his farm in the future.

The girls were delighted with their first triumph and were determined to carry on with all that good work but took all that success in their stride and it was admirable for their tender age. Even an adult at that juncture would have his head and ego inflated. Sohini was already on a path which spurts people to become leaders of their own communities but she was not thinking on those lines and did not want to be cast in that role. She was happy doing something according to the dictates of her heart.

As they say, nothing succeeds like success. After her triumph with the farmer who was mistreating his ox, She was inclined to enlarge her campaign against other social injustices happening around her. She was not simply a do- gooder as people assumed but her sympathies went for all victims of social injustices. She saw that landless labourers and the so-called lower classes of the society being treated like dirt by the rich and the powerful. She observed that some social classes had a tough time in the society as they were always treated like animals. The people, who did all the dirty work for the society, were considered as dirty themselves and they were called *bhangis* . Their place was not in the village but outside the village and where they lived in dilapidated huts, being a no go area for the higher classes of the village. Even if they touched a high caste person from the village accidentally, it was considered a great sin as their soul and body had been polluted by that touch and they had to purify themselves by going through the ritual of taking numerious baths.

Among the brahmin priest it was common practice that all their food was to be prepared only by another brahmin cook, otherwise being polluted it was not fit for consumption. This lower strata was not allowed to worship in the temples belonging to higher castes. Some people took this custom to the extreme, that they even thought themselves polluted when a shadow of a bhangi fell upon them. They had to purify themselves through bathing and washing constantly.

Sohni took up their cause and used it to visit their houses and listened to their grievances and helped them monetarily as much as she could. Initially people frowned upon her and thought her a misguided female but slowly she won the heart of other social reformers and various village dignitaries. She knew it was a hard fight against the entrenched prejudices of the people, which have entered into the sub- consciousness of the people. It was better to do something positive then simply ignore it.

 Soon a second front was opened as she took the cases of the low paid landless labourers to the justice authorities and the complaints of their treatments at the hand of the rich farmers. Her reputation established thus, spread far and wide and thus she became a sort of heroine for the masses.

It could be observed that such selfless action ushers in new conceptions of both mind and body. Without the initial push, the mind remained inert and tried to settle into comfortable illusion of non-action and slowly lost any taste for some positive action then lack of energy
Production of such a downward trend set in and the mind stopped being creative in any sense of the word. It seemed that this happened to Sohni when she took action and a stand against the cruelty to animals. She was on her initially but was joined by other sensible people who helped her and the good vibes of the mind were translated into action, new directions of sensibilities came into being then.

In The Days of Love

Conjecturing on it further, it might have been the dawn of human consciousness through the media of action. According to scientific research, human beings were evolved in Africa from the chimps and that took some millions of years. Continent of Africa used to be a very fertile land with plenty of rains and vegetation and the chimps lived happily, mostly on the trees as they could find all their requirements there with plenty of leaves and fruits to eat. There was no point for them to come down as there were plenty of predators lurking around in the undergrowth on the land beneath.

There used to be a large land mass at the south people and in time it broke into fragments, due to earth's rotation and these fragments began to move northwards. One of fragments was the continental of India and which took millions of years for it to travel north until it collided with continent of Asia and this impact was tremendous and catastrophic. It pushed against the Asian land mass, and Himalyan mountains were born and which began to grow taller and taller. And is still growing.

The monsoon currents used to flow freely bring plenty of rain and wet weather to Africa as it flew northwards from the southern seas but when the Himalyas began to grow to enormous heights, they obstructed the free flow of moisture laden air currents and consequently there were less and less flow across Africa and its climate began to change to a drier conditions. Abundance of vegetations and tree growths began to get dwindled. The creatures living on the trees could not find enough food to fill their stomachs and in order to survive they had to come down to ground level, to find enough food.

As they began to move along the ground through tangled vegetation and other obstacles, they found it hard to walk on all fours and some of the creatures took to walking on twos and these began to develop into proper legs and feet. The other two began to change into arms and legs as they were free of the exertion from walking. The leg and hand shape began to change under pressure from brain as to find new use of fingers and it proved to be a successful innovation. The fingers became a great instrument for making and using tools to tackle those jobs, which they were unable to do before. The use of finger brought innovatory actions into prominence and with the new understanding; the brain began to develop under the impetuous of action.

The actions of the fingers and the body had a direct effect on centers of the brain which became engaged in finding new ways of doing things and surmounting obstacle on the way and thus a dawn of intelligence and consciousness was born and slowly developed into human consciousness and the animal awareness took a new form. This innovatory mind ushered in a new mode of acquiring intelligence by exertion of body and Various other faculties were developed.

Chapter Three

When Sohni was little she was very fond of listening to stories told by a good story teller. She was inventing simple story herself and told them around to the amusements of companions and other adults including her parents. Her father was delighted and encouraged her to recite some stories about the farm animals. She invented a story about her favourite ox and in which he was the chief character fighting against the exploitation of other farm animals by some cruel farmer. She recited the story at her farm during the meal break and invited all the farm hands and other labourers from neighbouring farms. She was a delightful teller of tales; with her cute face and simple language to which simple folk could tune to and much appreciate it. Her father could not contain himself with delight, hugged and kissed her calling her an angel who was born to his family for giving comfort and joy to everybody at large.

Soon she joined the local primary school for her elementary education and where the teacher was an excellent fellow, well liked both by children and their parents. One day Sohni requested the teacher to tell the class some interesting story. The teacher was taken back as no one had made such a request before and felt embarrassed in front of children, as he was not a great storyteller and did not want to look foolish in front of children. But the children joined a course in unison 'Tell us a story! Tell us a story!' they shouted and the teacher realized that he could not get out of it. He could not give them story out of cuff at that moment but promised that he would tell them a story the following week.

He went home looking a bit worried and his wife saw it and asked him the reason for it and then he told her the reason. The wife told him not to worry unduly about it, as she would consult her sister was an expert in these matters and she would find a solution to his problem concerned. The woman concerned took delight in such matters and was sure you would find a truly strange story soon, to satisfy the demand of the children at the school. She gathered around all her friends and told them that she would be coming round to visit her who had a story up their sleeves would be forced to recite one.

On the visits, she listened to all the narrated stories but found one or two stories intriguing and which she wrote it down and came around to her sister's house and narrated the ones she liked best. The schoolmaster was keen on one story and noted it down in his own hand and corrected it to give it a nice finishing touch. The teacher was happy that he had somehow had managed to acquire a story to tell the children at the school as he had promised and thus save his face in front of them

When he went returned to school on the following Monday and informed the kids that he had a story up his sleeve and that they had to keep the Friday free off other engagements as he was going to tell them a nice and strange story. As the children became excited, it was time to cajole them to do extra work on the other days of the week and the children agreed to do so.

At mid morning all the children gathered in the classroom and made themselves comfortable and their faces showed excitement and eagerness for the story, to be told soon.

The teacher came and sat in front and cleared his throat.

'Is it a long story because we like long story?' Sohni asked in anticipation

'I am going to tell you that.' The teacher replied

In The Days of Love

'Why not?' a little boy asked

'What is the use of telling you a story, if you knew the answer to it. I want to keep you in suspense. So it will become more exciting.'

'But what sort of story is it? Is it a scary story?' asked a girl

The teacher smiled at the curiosity of his pupils.

'It will be a strange tale which will tell you something about the world in which we live.'

At last the teacher came to that moment when he was going to start his tale.

'There was a young boy who lived in a town not very far from our village. His life was not a happy one and his name was Daljeet and often pondered on his miserable life. One day Daljeet sat on his bed and reflected on his life. He realized that his life had been a tragedy as when he was only two years old his father died of an unknown illness. He could not remember him, not even a hazy recollection of him. He had a sister and a brother too and he could remember those but sadly they were taken away by the some unknown disease too and no one could do anything about it.'

'Poor! Poor! People' said the children with sadness on their eyes.

'His sick mother was lying on a bed next to him and coughing and having difficulty in breathing. Why his life turned out to be such bad and full of misery of all kinds. They were living in a small rented house of two rooms, with a small courtyard attached.

He used to go to school when his mother was well and was also doing part time job. He had to withdraw from class eight at the school as he had to look after her sick mother and also because he could not afford the fees for his education. In order keep himself and his mother alive, he was always on lookout for any job, menial or otherwise, he could find. He went to work for the local sweetmeat maker where he had to clean and wash all the equipment associated with that trade. Big greasy cauldron or karahis in which the various sweets were made and cooked. Wheat, maize and gram flour were used and made into a barter and from which different combinations took place, cooked in hot oils or in sweet sugary liquids. This all left a lot of mess and grease in nooks and corners of the vessels used and removing these was a backbreaking and arm stressing job.

The left overs of grease, sticky sweets and remnants of cooked oil, which left overnight, created a hell of bad smell from the putrefied matter. It was a highly unpleasant job but he had to do it in order to earn some money. Halwai's bottom rung employees had to start like this and to slowly work their ways up. Other part of his job consisted of keeping the premises clean and tidy. He started his work very early in the mornings when it was still dark and went home till the evening darkness came over. He was given free food for himself and her sick mother and he went home during mid-daybreak for one hour. He was glad to have any sort of job as long as it kept the wolf away from the door and save him from starvation.

Diwali came and that was the best season for selling the sweets. He was glad to have such break from his dull routine. During those festivities of Diwali the sale increased ten folds. He tried to forget about his life to join in the festivities. It was a time to forget and enjoy life because he knew that soon it would be over and his sad little life will return. For the time being his employer had plenty of overtime available for the staff to prepare extra goodies for the festival day as the sale of sweet would go enormously.

It took hours to arrange the trays of sweets around the front stall in an ascending order of steps. It looked marvelous display with varieties of sweets and savories. Jalebis, gulam Jamans, badam burfies, peras. kalakands, basins, rasgulas etc. He was afforded the privilege of covering each tray of sweets with gold and silver leafs. These costly leafs came into sort of booklets with the thin delicate metallic things pressed between paper leaves in. These were so delicate that even an accidental breath flow blew them away. When he was covering the sweets, he felt like an artist creating some delicate compositions. He enjoyed this sophisticated job and was loathed to go back to his job of utensil cleaning.

As time went he slowly worked his way up to be one of the assistants of the halwai and he was now in his twenties.

 It so happened that the economic situation in the country began to deteriorate due to high inflation and soon the government raised the interest rates. The people and businesses that had borrowed heavily could not afford to repay the loans and as they defaulted, the banks lost on their investments and so a general recession ensued. The sweetmeat seller could not afford to keep all his workers on the books and so most of the employees including Daljeet were made redundant. It is said that bad luck comes in droves; he had his worries not account only for lack of money but also regarding the deteriorating health of his mother.

 The condition of his mother began to get worse and she began to spit great amount of phlegm and sometime with traces of blood in her spit. She began to feel weaker and weaker each day and one day when he came home during lunchtime with some food, he found her dead. He ran to the neighbours crying and screaming for help. All gathered around and mourned for his dead mother and tried to console him as much as they could.

They soon found out that his household was poverty stricken and could not even afford to buy the provisions and food enough to fill the stomach, not to mention the funeral and other expenses to be incurred

They took pity on him, arranged at their own expenses the funeral for her mother. He saw the funeral pyre burning before him and then collected the ashes. The neighbours arranged the journey for him, when he had to go to a holy place with bundle of ashes and cast out these into the waters of a river considered to be holy. Neighbours soon realized that the grief he had to bear was great and for such a person of delicate sensitivity and was overwhelming. In order to help him emotionally, they suggested for him to go to a famous temple afterwards and where god willing, he might be able to recover from his tragedy and find some peace.

He went to the holy place in the mountains in order to cast away the ashes of her dead mother and felt that suddenly he had lost all his contacts with the outside world and could no longer establish any emotional ties with it. He became a man without any human connections and without any memories, just some sort of robotic entity without any convictions or any desire for action. He felt into a deep depression and of body and soul. Somehow he dragged himself out of that mood and started his journey to the city of Mansrover with its famed golden temple. The bus was overcrowded but he squeezed himself in and found a space to sit. He had no concern for himself anymore or for his comfort as such it was not a problem; He got down at the bus terminal and took a rickshaw to the golden temple. The rickshaw driver was jostling its way through the crowded streets full of people and vehicles-other rickshaws, tongas, scooters, hand carts, bullock carts, bicycles and whatnots but he took little notice of those milling crowds. The rickshaw took him to a stand near the temple and from there he had to make his own way walking through a labyrinth of narrow winding Streets.

The temple was surrounded by a high wall with four tall doors at each entrance, each symbolizing the four points of space- east, west, north and south and the four races of men to seek shelter. There were marbled stairs leading to the high entrance and slowly he entered the huge door. The numbness of his mind and the gloominess suddenly lifted and he felt entering a new world where even all his dark sorrows became of lighter shade. The golden temple impressed him with its great splendour and charm and he gave himself completely to it. Moisture began to film his eyes, washing away the encrusted dirt of all his past. He spent the whole day contemplating that splendour and returned to his place in the evening.

After returning home, he felt even extremely lonely and in order to get away, he tried to find a job but no one wanted him. Soon someone he knew was offered a night watchman's job, which he turned down as of unsociable hours. As Daljeet was desperate, he took the job himself with resident's association; they wanted someone honest and reliable to do the job of guarding their homes against petty thieves and burglars at night.

His duty started at 10pm and lasted up to 6am the following morning. Each hour of his duty he went round the assigned streets shouting "Khabardar! Be aware! The hour is -- o'clock." And each time he shouted, "Be aware" People felt safe in their beds that someone was there guarding their properties and also they were kept informed of the time at each hour of the night. He took his charpoy or rope-stringed bed with him and rested on it between the rounds. He was alone but persisted with his loneliness. After a certain period a stray dog began to visit him, sitting there looking at him and in their loneliness the sight of each other gave solace to both.

He started bringing food for the dog and encouraged by it, the dog stayed there the whole night during his duty hours. He was glad to have some company. But it was only during winter period that they needed a watchman and his period of employment came to an end, after few months, when summer arrived.

There was nothing left to hold him there as all his emotional ties with that place broke and he sought the place where he could find some meaning to his existence. He headed for the golden temple again. He boarded the bus and tried to join in the hub of humanity with their laughter and talks, to forget himself. He found a place near the vehicle window to sit and look out and lost himself in the panorama of passing sights. There were tall tree planted on both sides of the road casting pleasant shadows from their leafy tops. Beyond the trees he could glimpse fertile fields planted with all sorts of crops, green trees with various formations of hue and colour. Here and there a farmer was working in the fields accompanied by his dog. Children were playing their noisy games busy in their frolics unaware of any future to come with all his worries, which the passing time always brought.

He reached the city and hired a rickshaw to take him to the temple and was delighted to behold its golden domes and tall gates again. He went around on the marbled borders after leaving his shoes; he walked bare footed on the marbled that surrounded the pool. The marble under his feet felt cool and soothing. He bought some parsad from the stall to be taken to the temple as an offering.

The temple was situated amid a beautiful lake; he walked on a causeway connecting to it and for few minutes stood there admiring the view. He went to the central temple and gave offerings of parsad to the priest and the priest added it to the common collection, from which the priest distributed to all the incoming devotees and pilgrims.

He sat there listening to hymns of guru, which communicated with him at a personal level. He went to langar, the common kitchen and ate the offered food. He was fully satisfied and did not want to move to anywhere else. He spread his blanket outside the gates and soon was in a deep sleep. The keeper of the door found him sleeping, his sad face and twisted body inducing compassion in the passersby. The keeper woke him up and took him to a vacant room in the complex and there he slept again.

When the doors opened, he was anxious to set o the marbled steps of the pool and to wonder on its ethereal beauty. The sound of the sweet hymns reverberated in the space. He extended his bare arm and touched the water. The dazzling golden reflections of the temple became visible and as he touched it, they multiplied in thousand fragments. He felt something unknown, beyond his comprehension- something vast but still humanly soothing.

He was in two worlds at the same time, one of the golden domes and one of the ethereal reflections. He would spend his days contemplating them.'

Chapter Four

After spending the night at the temple, Karan was on move again. He was under order from the temple priest to leave the following morning and thus had no choice but to abandon his abode for the night. He would have like to stay under that roof for another night, to think out his problems.

He was not sure about his future and had no idea about his forward journey either- where it would lead into? Perhaps into the unknown and all he could do was simply to trust his strivings. He decided to walk a pathway down-stream like a rudderless boat without any direction, just a vehicle drifting downstream with the flow of the current. He was simply to follow his instincts.

As always grass was greener on the other side and he thought that territory on opposite bank of the river looked promising and might provide him with some crumbs of good fortune. He just wanted to keep to his present path until a suitable point of crossing came along. The river was swollen with the recent heavy rains and difficult to cross on one's own, swimming across was impossible: he needed a ferry to cross.

Eventually he hit a big village but with all the facilities of a small town. It had a unique atmosphere with lots of hustle and bustle. He walked through it to taste its atmosphere and then headed for the waterfront again where numbers of ferries were moored ready for crossing the river. It had lively crowds with plenty of people ready for crossing to other shores mingling with people coming from the opposite direction. There were farmers with tied bundles on their heads, women with small children dressed in all regalia, families with pets and goats and snake charmers playing their *beens* with shinning cobras dancing to their movements. It was an entertainment in itself to look at that spectacle of people.

In The Days of Love

He sat there to watch people coming and going and noticed the ferrymen charging money to the people before entering their ferries. As he did not have much money on his person, he was reluctant to approach them. He felt a pal of gloom coming over him and his loneliness surrounded him again on all sides and everything became a dark unknown through which his feeble mind could not penetrate. What was he living for anyway? This question became larger and larger and then engulfed him expelling out all his energies and zest of living, from his mind. As a child he used to be surrounded by human warmth and protection loved ones gave him and what now? A cold despair was there chilling his heart and entrails.

But that is the destiny of all living beings? That was the question reverberating through his mind to which he had no answer. He felt useless and unwanted in the whole world. After all it was full of people and other living beings, somehow he had to find a connection to those alive, and otherwise there was no hope for him. He realized that such gloomy thoughts were only good for that despondency which only directed him to seek solace in the lap of an easeful death but then it was just a common way fit for a coward - an easy way out of miseries of living. Only if he could lift his gloom he may be able to withstand the onslaughts of such crippling thoughts.

Hours passed in such reveries but suddenly he came to his present surroundings, he felt week and realized that he had not eaten for sometime. He searched through his pocket and found few pieces of coins left over and bought some tea and bread to appease his hunger.

The evening was descending and sky became afired with setting sun, the sky was like a big stretched canvas on which somebody had brushed in a mixture of black, red and yellow to express multitude of inner desires, mostly un-fulfilled with expressions torturing on the edge of agony. Some foreshadows of doom concealed within dying day –a path leading towards life's end.

He looked for a place to spend the night and saw a beautiful boat moored around the corner, it was empty and he decided to take advantage. There was a comfortable make shift bed within its shed and when he lay on it he found it comfortable. Slowly the density of darkness increased and men and beasts took shelter in it for the night and everything became still and quite, except the sounds of lapping water.

He was woken suddenly by the sounds of voices and tried to comprehend the situation, through his half closed sleepy eyes and dormant consciousness. He saw a troupe of girls on the boat and a pretty girl acting as their spokeswoman. It was Sohni who had come to enquire as who was sleeping in her boat and occupying her private bed. Though she was considered as sensible by her friends in all situations but now she was in a jittery mood incensed by a man who dared to sleep in her very bed.

As Karan tried to get up to face her, she pushed him aside with a violence that surprised her friends. They had never seen her in such an agitated state before. Karan was stung by her beauty and overpowered by her personality and felt unable to return any violence towards her. She demanded to know why he had committed such a heinous act; he tried to mumble out an explanation as to his ignorance about the boat being her property. In her heart she was stung too by his good looks and this annoyed her greatly. No man had such a powerful effect on her and it made her loose self-control.

It was beyond her rational mind to control her temper and she lashed out, slapping Karan in his face. It had a devastating effect on Karan. He thought himself innocent of any wrongdoing and as a homeless person just wanted to spend the night in a vacant boat. There was no harm in it, he was not committing any criminal act or trying to steal her boat.

He had been driven out of his house, lost his beloved father, hungry and homeless and now that was the last insult to his person. He tried to suppress the deep wounds inflicted on his heart but it was too much for his soul. Tears began to roll down from his eyes.

Sohni became confused too and regretted the use of violence on an innocent man. She did not know what to do and just stormed out leaving Karan and her own friends there.

Under the violence of last incident Karan became even more depressed, stepped out of the boat and just entered the river and went forward into the deeper water and when the girls saw him, they just screamed and shouted and told him to come back and not to take his life by drowning. They held their hands together to reach him and dragged him out of water onto the dry bank and where he collapsed. He was shivering and mumbling incoherently. Someone brought him a blanket and covered him. One of the girls sent for her father and when he came, they removed him to their house and put him on a clean bed. He was delirious and they noticed that he had not eaten properly for some time and thus prepared some hot soup and vegetables for him and spoon-fed him. Eventually a deep sleep came over him.

Sohni was extremely upset and as she reached home, she did not know what to do next and in her great confusion went into the kitchen and put a pot on the fire and poured some water into it. Why was she boiling the water? She did not have a clue. It was just to take her mind off her embarrassment about that recent incidence. She did not want to remember or reason out anything as to why she hit that young man at her boat in spite that he never raised a hand against her or became rude in manners towards her. In her heart of heart she felt even attracted to him and sensed something deep within him and it was causing her pain. She should not have treated him so harshly; he might not have known that the boat belonged to her. She had always helped people and had been kind to them. Why, why then? Everybody had looked up to her and she was even the leader of the group of her friends. Was it simply a mixture of his attraction to her and a sort of disobedience towards her? Now she was hurt and deeply regretted her action. She had never been before in that sort of situation where she just lashed out at people and it happened due to lack of understanding on her part. It was simply awful.

She was growing up and had his first experience of an attraction towards opposite sex. She had heard things about love and relationship but never had experienced herself. She had read some love stories in the books or heard songs that were full of wonders and pangs of love but these were only what had happened to other people and it was always a sort of entertainment talking about it, to pass the time among her friends. Was it happening to her now? She was not sure of it and if it did, what was that love after all? She was not sure even of that. Two people looked at each other and their eyes met and suddenly a mutual feeling had sprung between them, which could be called some sort of attraction between the sexes. May be it was some sort of life force which bound two people together instantly. That in a way was the curtailment of their freedom but in spite that understanding she still wanted to savour that feeling repeatedly and wanted to lose yourself into a world which coagulates two people in a sort of spiritual embrace, in an unknown land which had different laws of behaviour.

With that strange feeling of love for another, an emotion sprung over her-that of pity and compassion about her victim. She felt uncomfortable with her act of slapping him. It was damn cruel of her to hit a grown up man in the face like the punishment handed to a naughty child at a school by the teacher. She spent restless day and night thinking about it but could not come to any conclusion but her repentance was deep. She was sorry for her act and wanted to undo it somehow by either apologizing to Karan or by compensating him in kind, for all the emotional harms done to him.

When she woke up early in the morning, she felt tired and drained and thought that a morning walk would do her good and might even restore her sagging spirits. She walked out of the village and soon was near the waterfront and she looked at the meandering waters. The river was in no hurry to perform its task of flowing and took everything in its stride. How wise was the river, she thought and she might follow its example. She began to walk on the embankment with quickened steps.

The sun was slowly rising from the depths of the river waters and causing a turbulence and clash of the colours on the watery surface of the river which was glowing in all its glory mingling shadows and reflected sunshine into myriads of patterns and if one had the capacity to lose into those emotions, one could forget oneself momentarily and find relief from vagaries of one's life. After few miles on her morning walk, she turned her steps homeward.

When she was near the village, she realized that in her emotional tumult she had been walking at a great speed and covered the distance rapidly and it was still early in the morning. She did not want to return home so soon and get entangled in her emotional complexes again. She would spend her time in swimming and bathing in the river. She entered the river and took a step forward into its depth and the water felt cool and made her shiver. She took a dip into it and it cleared her mind slightly and it was a refreshing change. She took another dip and saw through the water the zigzagging picture of the sky and the banks, in a land of shimmering world.

She stayed in the water for some time, then came out and lay on the grassy verges and the sun sent its warm rays to caress her body leading to the movements for life- that life was all around her- in the sky, on the earth, in the gentle breeze, in the melodious songs of the birds, in the gentle lapping of waves. It was glorious to be alive again, why was she afraid of her own emotions? The river had taught her a lesson in the art of living and she would carry that lesson further into her life. She would be a courageous soul and would think about her problems in the future with a cool outlook. She returned home refreshed.

*

Karan slowly was regaining his lost strength, n being looked after by some kind souls of the village. Since his father died, he did not have luxury of such privileges accorded to him and consequently he was overwhelmed and could not envisage why any person would be caring for him? He was useless fellow, hated by all and sundry- his brothers and even by the temple priest. He did not have any property of his own to show off, practically bankrupt and being a burden on everybody and could not even earn his crust like any other honest man. He was simply useless

Such thoughts depressed him greatly and increased his hatred of himself and for life in general. The only ray of sunshine left in his life was the troupe of girls who surrounded him as he was captivated by their tenderness and excellent marks of beauty. It happens sometime that even in the midst of hunger and poverty, a certain kind of beauty can uplift your soul in spite of the dictates of the logic, which points out to the opposite of your logic. The girls were encouraging him to get up and walk and accompany them to the banks of the river but which he was reluctant to do.

In The Days of Love

They found a wooden flute on his person and deduced that he was a musician and it was a spur on their parts to coax him to play something for them. Even the elders encouraged him to take up his flute again to entertain the people around him. As without any thing to do the unoccupied brain gets lazy and the mind can started going funny, inventing all kinds of imaginary things- dark depressing hallucinatory images.

Encouraged Karan took up his flute again and began blowing into it but without any rhythm or plan and wanted to throw it in the river but then a thought struck him that he should express his real feeling into his music. His heart was full of despondency and pain, which he tried to express and lo a tragic tune was born and issued forth from his flute and Karan, realized that despite its tragic undertones, it was a beautiful tune and began to develop that theme into more elaborate variations. He noticed that some children and adults gathered round him listening and encouraged him to play more.

Slowly more and more melodies began to pour and a sea of melodies was a gathering within his instrument and he had just to pick one and it poured through without any effort on his part. There were so many hidden niches in his deep psyche to which he had no access in his normal consciousness but with so many drastic happening in his life, music had awakened to solace his wounded self and such was happening to him now. In our normal living that tends towards utilitarianism such musing did not have much use in battles of life but when something happen beyond his control there was an outpourings of hidden abilities. What was the melody anyhow? These were invisible messengers and who could gauge their depths? Those were only meant to be listened to by people and there were no rules or any coded structures and the amazing thing was that each melody was different from one another. The real miracle was that with seven notes one could create infinity of tunes and melodies. These musical compositions had an inexhaustible source at their being and even when one played a similar composition, their effect was different each time.

Against his expectations he sensed that his soul had found a path of recovery and healing. He took up his musical creation with a more determined mode. He was thankful to his protectors for looking after him and for feeding him and thought himself under their debt of kindness. He would surely pay them back for this perhaps someday in the future. Firstly he had to find a job to earn his living -- he could not live forever on the charity of others. He consulted various people but found that he had not much experience either in farming or business. You needed money to run a business and which he simply did not possess. The only thing he was capable of was either playing his flute or grazing the cattle.

He decided to go for the grazing, as it was a big village with plenty of cows and buffaloes, owned by the farmers and other villagers but his problem was as how to approach a suitable person to organize the thing. He thought of himself as not capable of bargaining for his wages or fees charged for each individual animal taken out for grazing. His friends suggested that he should start shepherding a few head of the cattle belonging to them and for the time being he could stay with them as they would provide him with shelter and food, and Karan readily accepted it .He started by taking out half a dozen cattle out for the grazing. After breakfast each day, he went around various houses to collect the cattle, rounded them up and went to the wilderness outside the village where he could find enough grass for the cattle to feed on.

Firstly the cattle did not take to him easily as he presented them a threat and just like human they did not trust him sufficiently to obey his instructions. These were running about and breaking all the group formation and it took him considerable time and headache to bring them together as a group. It happened for first few days but afterwards he noticed that they were becoming more docile and responding to his instructions. As he was a gentle person, the cattle soon sensed that he was not going to do any harm. They started coming to him for little bit of love and a pat on their foreheads. They seemed to like that interaction with human being as the pets in a household do and behaved towards their caring owners.

Sohni was still suffering from her pains and embarrassment and wanted to somehow resolve the situation as soon as possible and it was sapping her inner strength. She wanted some piece of advice from someone to do some sort of reconciliation with Karan. She realized that he must have suffered from her rash act. But there were difficulties in the process of reconciliation, as she did not want to admit that she had done any wrong. She was a proud woman and it was very painful for her to admit her mistake in front of other people. Her friends had not visited her for few days, so she must had done something bad to put them off. Lastly she sent one of her servant to inform the friends that she was sick and needed their help.

Hearing that all her friends rushed to her, as they loved her dearly. Slowly she disclosed her inner tumult and asked for their help as to resolve the situation for her. They realized that in order to resolve it, they had to arrange a rendezvous between two parties without their knowledge. They hatched a plot to send her with a nice meal to Karin instead of a servant who usually supplied him previously. They told her that her friends would be going for a picnic outside the village and each one should join and bring some prepared meals to share.

On the appointed morning, all the girls gathered at Sohni's house with all sorts of eateries and fruits and started their walk to a suitable picnic spot. All were in a jolly mood and giggly with a hint of mischief in their eyes. They wore long colourful robes with matching scarves. Everybody noticed them in streets of the village. They were like a bunch of butterflies fluttering in the cool breeze of the morning. It was a sight for the sore eyes, all that youthful grace and charm. Seeing them the old folks felt a pang of envy for their lost youth. The girls were happy except Sohni who had still trepidations about her actions over the past few days.

The girl soon found a secret spot for their picnic knowingly and it was near where Karan was grazing his cattle. They spread themselves on the grass- indulging in all the vagaries of youth, they slapped gently and teased each other about their lovers and talked about other young men whom they fancied. Eventually they had some refreshments, rested and proposed a game of hide and seek. Sohni did not show any enthusiasm for that game but was persuaded by her friends to join in the fun as for some physical activity. The girl knew that Karan was grazing on the other side of the fence, where their game was being conducted.

By a process of choosing the short straw, Sohni was assigned the girl to be the seeker and the other girl as hiders. She had to put on a blindfold herself and give other girls enough time to hide and when they called that they were ready, Sohni took off her blindfold and started searching for all the hiders, walking in the directions of deemed voices. She crossed the fence along the field and came to an open field full of fresh grass and observed a shepherd with some cattle. He was sitting under a tree playing his flute.

It was a pleasant and soothing sound flowing over the open grass lands and scattering its musical message through its notes, notes of sadness and notes of happiness, molded into an interesting composition. The melody was full of pathos, pathos of loss and such melodies touched the human heart deeply and it seemed that sweetest were those, which told about the saddest things. She forgot about the game and began to move towards the sound of flute. She saw a man wearing long robes and lemon green turban. Suddenly a recollection came to her and which stopped her in her tracks. Was it the man whom she had slapped and booted out of her boat? Yes it was the same man. She could not face confronting him alone and just stood there with her mind numbed.

Karan was the first one to see her and in spite of the bitterness of the last episode, he wanted to say something to the girl who was standing there dumb and embarrassed. He came near her

'Hello Sohni, It is nice to see you again.' He said looking at her enchanting face.

'It is nice to see you too again' Sohni managed to blurt it out.

'Are you well?'

'No, I have been unwell. During last few days I had bad dreams for the bad things I had done for which I am sorry. God forbid, I am ashamed of my actions especially against you.' Sohni at last managed to say something about her grief to get it out of her chest and that had been bothering her a great deal for the last few days.

' Do not worry much on my account, I am getting used to such harsh treatments. Since I left my home after the death of my father, it had been bad sailing for me and my father was the only person who showed any love and affection for me.' Karan said truthfully, expressing his pent up grief without any malice in his tone.

'Do not worry too much about your life. I am sure you will soon find someone who will love and care for you. You are a handsome man with good heart to go with it'

At these words, Karan was truly touched. He wanted to say something pleasing in return, for all the appreciations offered by Sohni but could not formulate words to express it. In his clumsiness he caught hold of her hand, brought it to touch his forehead and then gently kissed it. Although he was afraid of her sharp temper, he was glad that he had dared to do that.

At that moments all sohni's friends emerged from their hiding places laughing, came together and all embraced the couple and showed their joy by praising and shouting for both of them. They were overjoyed at the reconciliation.

When Sohni returned home, she was in a great mood as the meeting with Karan had affected her positively. All her burdens of the past had been lifted and replaced by a gentle torture, which may be called love. The exchange of energies between male and female has its own subtle powers and that was hard to define, those could only be experienced and not defined and if given as too much explanation could rob it of its depths. When you liked someone, you wanted to do something special for that person and Sohni was keen to help him in finding some permanent job as to earn some kind of living. She thought about some suitable job for him and that were heard to envisage, as Karan seemed to be totally disinterested in any routine job. She had not found a person of such low ambitions and devoid of any wishes for acquiring worldly goods or look forward to a future, which appealed to people of normal bent.

She consulted her friends and they advised her that as he was doing some grazing job with a few cattle and if he were to be employed by a big farmer to look after the animals, that would be more useful. Sohni thought about their big farm and resolved to speak about it to her father. One evening when her father was free she asked:

'Father, we have so many animals, we should not employ someone to look after them.'

'As a matter of fact we do and I was thinking on the same line, have you someone in mind?' Father enquired

'Yes I have a good person in mind, I do not know much about his background but he seems to be a kind person and a hard working one.'

'How long have you known him?'

'Not long, I have met him only twice.'

'Is he a good looking fellow'? The father teased her

Sohni blushed and his father noticed it.

'Don't you worry, ask him to come and see me tomorrow evening.'

A message was sent via a messenger to Karan as to come and see sohni's father.

Karan was very apprehensive about the message and he thought about his last meeting with Sohni and he went over all the details, over and over. He must have committed some blunder resulting in a wrong behaviour, he should not have caught hold of her hand and then kissed it. Without thinking and on a spur of moment he made a rude blunder and now he had to suffer the consequence of that act. Sohni must have informed about it to his father and in annoyance he had called him to see him. At last he was making some friend in the village but now he would be punished, sacked and driven out of village again. He kept rolling in his bed whole night and did not get any sleep. In the morning he thought about running away from the village but in the end he decided to face the music and went to see the father.

The father was sitting in the main courtyard and when Karan was shown in, he was offered a seat and which he accepted with thanks. All the time he was anxiously glancing at his face to detect any trace of anger there but he found none and this assured him. He was offered a portion of evening meal, which he refused as it was customary, a sign of refinement and good manners but accepted when the father insisted upon it second time. Sohni wanted to serve the special guest herself, which surprised her father but he accepted it in good humour. After the meal, the father asked him:

'My daughter speaks highly of you. Give me some background of your family.'

'I came from a good peasant family with brothers and sisters and shared the burden of farming with my father. My father was a grand man, being kind to everyone. He was specially loving and protective towards me.' Karan replied.

'What happened after the death of your father.'?

'Unfortunately no one else liked me in the family and I was driven out.'

'But why so?'

'My brothers and sisters did not like me very much stating that I was naïve and not clever enough with my hands or brain, in a sort of worldly way. Further I was not ambitious enough either to acquire more land for the family or plan something to increase the fortune and wealth of the family.'

'It seems a sad story.'

In The Days of Love

'One day my father did not feel well and took to the bed. I was heartbroken and left all my chores to look after him all hours of day and night. He lingered on for another six months. It was a pitiable sight to see him with his body reduced to skeleton and when he died, the entire world around me collapsed. No one beside him has ever loved me.' As Karan spoke, the father was touched and promised to help him to get to his feet.

There were plenty of animals in Sohni's household, which needed to be looked after and taken care of and it was a good opportunity to employ Karan in that capacity. She and her father agreed on this idea. They decided to put their plan into practice at the earliest opportunity. She took upon herself to familiarize Karan into new setup. She introduced him to her favourite oxen, cows and buffaloes and to whom she had given individual loving names. Karan was greatly impressed by her inner gentleness and love towards the animals.

Amid their vast tract of land, there was a picturesque but depilated hut, which was inhabited and it was offered to Karan as his living quarters. He greatly appreciated it and accepted it and he would move into at the end of the month. In the meantime, her father took him to a tailor to have some new dresses made for him, to which Karan objected as he was reluctant to accept so many favours showered on him by Sohni's household but in the end had to accept it as not to annoy every one with his rash behaviour again.

It seemed that things all around turned out for better for all the parties concerned. It was a heartwarming and joyous occasion for everybody.

Nihilism confronts us all the in our struggles for living. It is the meaninglessness that breaks the back of every aspirant in the art of living but the idea of a meaningful life is surprisingly elusive. The quest for meaningfulness is relational and a life has meaning by virtue of its relation to something else and in this case Kiran had to deal with the problem of relationship. When his father was alive, his life was full with that loving relationship being his favourite youngest child. When he died that link was broken and with that collapse of any meaningful relation, there was no one to replace that.

For most people a profession or mode of living to earn their crust was normally the second best thing. A profession was a good choice not only because it was interesting or lucrative but also because it related one to the family tradition but in his case the brothers had already edged him out of the family farming traditions. His temperament did not help as it was tended towards inward as opposed to routine farming work involving rotational crop sowing, harvesting and other such physical work. In such work you need a traditional outlook that got things done without any application of intellect. He would feel trapped and would become a sort of prison to him. A poetical temperament needs a constant escape from such routine work and a constant creation out of inner impulses.

A life could also be meaningful by securing a different kind of relation with his surrounding or environments and to that he was partially successful. He could relate to the fields, earth and animals and that brought a meaning into his life but still his father was a catalyst around which these secondary values evolved and when he died his world collapsed and with it all those secondary relationship Once more he was rudderless with no practical skill to save him from the jaws of despair.

To some the magnitude of the universe and our place in it might be beneficial in tackling the problem of despair but few had the capacity to comprehend it. The magnitude of the universe could be such that no human life could ever hope to make much difference to its inner workings when you could arrive at an understanding that a meaningful life could be lived without any dependency on relationship. Such an attitude could make you to look for uncharted territory of mind as if your life could offer little to the overall universe, but could still manage a meaningfulness to your life i.e. of standing alone and having self-reliance when amazingly a new zest for living is born. Few could think on those lines and even fewer could act upon those, as most people wanted the surety of an authority whether it was religious, scientific or some words quoted by the celebrities of the history.

If you could stand your own ground in spite of what other people say or act, even a 'meaningless' life could be worth living but who could do that? The people could not live on convictions alone, which was a bare rock without any foothold and people needed the glue of emotions to fix their broken inner pieces. Such goals of love, emotional attachments, attachments to properties and money masks life worth living to the majority and inspired them to go on living and escape from the abyss of despair that yawns before and ignored by most.

Another sophisticated mode of mind could be created out of utter despair, as it might be possible. Even in the state of utter desperation a wisdom is born, a wisdom of transcendence in which old traditional values are cast aside and new spirit for freedom is born with its a courage of being, a courage related to some higher power to our ground of existence. But such power needed an iron will which wanted to succeed in spite of all the obstacles of emotional complexes which each human being carried within themselves but that Karan lacked.

Chapter Five

Karan was now employed by her father in the capacity of cowherd for the family and Sohni was appointed as his supervisor. She had to introduce him to his various duties, which he was to take on under her command.

Sohni had lovingly named all her household animals with individual names and Karan had to learn all these by heart but which turned out to be not such a difficult task. Secondly she had to instruct him regarding the eating habits of all the animals, which Karan thought was too much pampering of animals on her part.

After few days the situation settled down and a sort of intimacy developed between two of them and they began to become more familiar to each other and started to talk more freely among themselves. The last incidence of the boat was always at the back of his mind. One day Karan asked her:

'Why did you hit me on your boat where I was resting? I meant no harm.'

' I and my friends came on that day to bathe and all that bell tinkling around our anklets drew a crowd, which was so annoying to me. There was a guard to protect my boat from intruders and when I saw you lying in my boat, I was furious that somebody has defiled the very couch of mine on which I sometime sleep and my guard has allowed someone to sleep in the same bed. I thought that my privacy had been invaded.'

'What did you do then? Just slap me instead of explanation from your guard.'

In The Days of Love

'No I was so furious with my guard, Ludan and I advanced towards him and he got frightened and put his hands up, begging me not to hit him. He stated that giving shelter for the night to a homeless person was not such a crime and begged his forgiveness from me.'

'I see you forgave him but instead of it, poured all your anger on me.' Said Karan

'I would not have hit you, if you had begged for my forgiveness I needed to feel that my authority was respected.' Replied Sohni, trying to make an excuse for her rashness.

'But my dear lady! You did not give me a chance to do that.'

'I am sorry. I will recompense you for it with my love someday.' Blushingly Sohni replied.

Karan was so pleased with that reply and just when he wanted to take Sohni in his arms she ran away.

When Sohni reached home, his father asked her whether everything was in order, 'it could not be better' was her reply. She was elated and at the same time agitated and it seemed the first pangs of love were piercing her heart. When you fell in love, it was a strange feeling and there was nothing like it as to compare with your other experiences of the past. It was a sort of bitter sweet reverie. A sweet torture, which you want to abandon and not to abandon at the same time. The image of that beloved face got under your skin and you wanted to keep it there forever, enclosed within your being at all cost. You could ponder and think about it for ages and ages and still not come to its conclusion. Strange thing that love was. No wonder that musicians had composed endless songs on it and poets had delved into numerous verses. As they say about God whom people had tried to define for ages and ages but he still remained undefined and unsung. In order to catch a glimpse of divinity you may have to compose a new song each time and each would be a different sort of thing and even then you could not reach the end of that divinity.

Being a proud girl, she shied away from being dependent on any one else as she had always thought of herself as self sufficient and independent. And now she had to handle somehow her desire to love and to be loved by someone else and it was difficult for her. How long she could conceal her inner agony and ecstasy from the outside world and still pretend to be hale and hearty to the eyes of the world as if she had no care in the world. She decided that she would try to pretend as long as possible and see what happened afterwards.

As things resolved she went about her business pretending to be in control of all her emotions and did not show any trace of visible signs or any sentimental feelings. She dealt with everybody including Karan as a matter of routine in a full practical normal way. She avoided looking into his face while talking and did not allow herself any eye contact with him. She dealt with all the matter at hand factually in a natural way and if anyone needed any assistance, she would simply provide it without getting personally involved. She instructed Karan in all manners of animal husbandry to look after those creatures in an efficient manner as per her instructions provided. She entered daily reports in her procedural diaries and accounts ledger and presented these, at the end of each week, to his father for final scrutinisation.

His father was pleased and impressed with her work and the manner she dealt with day to day business of running the farm and also dealt with any complaint received in an efficient and courteous fashion.

Karan often saw her when being supervised at his duties as a cowherd but to him, Sohni seemed to have changed her attitude towards him to a more mechanical way, which hurt him greatly as he could not think of any annoying thing he might had done to upset her. He greatly admired her and her face and figure had impressed him greatly but why she had turned so indifferent towards him? He wanted to know. It was a heart-breaking time for him. She even would not look him in the eyes and or even to talk to him in a friendly tone, it was beyond him. He felt that he had fallen in love with that inscrutable girl and it was impossible to retrieve now from that position of entrenchment. When your affections were awakened you began to form a better and more beautiful picture of the person you are attached to .It may be a delusion on your part but that is the way things turned out and which he had to accept and endure.

 He began to blame himself and about the way he fell in love with a person who might not pay attention to him or say something through a meaningful glance .He thought he had at last found something to love and to admire and now it had turned out to be so different from his past experience.

He wanted to resolve that issue and thought a great deal about it and one day plucked enough courage to talk to one of the close friend of Sohni. He laid his heart bare before her and confessed that he had fallen for Sohni and her beauty and which had enchanted him and hurt his heart brutally but feared that she was no longer interested in him. That friend assured him that that was not the case and she advised him to communicate with her directly but he stated that he was afraid of her in any face to face encounter. Would she advise him an alternative course of action. She suggested that he should write a letter to her.

 He struggled over the format and contents of the letter. What should he write and how should he start it. He did not want to bare his heart completely as the lady concerned might ridicule his sentiments or just get annoyed and kick him out of his job which would be terrible blow as he was sick of being rejected by everyone. 'Dear so & so' seemed so conventional & flowery and also how could he address her as her dear when in truth she might not consider him 'a dear'. So he had to use another conventional form of addressing her as ' Dear Respectable Miss. Sohni'and thought that it was good enough for him.

So he started drafting the letter:

Dear Respectable Miss Sohni

Sat Siri Akaal

I have been on the verge of talking to you sometime during last few days but could
not bring myself to communicate with you in face to face encounter.

I hope you will not be annoyed to read this letter. If I cause you any anxiety or annoyance, please forgive me and destroy the letter immediately and that will be the end
of the matter.

Since I saw you first time, I have been struck by your beauty and I find you attractive as a woman is to a man but there is no hidden agenda underlining all that.

It seems that you have changed during past few days, as you seem so distant and indifferent towards me. I hope I have not done any stupid thing to annoy you.

If you allow me, I would like to see you and explain things in greater details.

Please grant me an opportunity to see you at an appointed time as convenient to you.

In The Days of Love

Your Obedient Servant.

Karan.

He kept the letter to himself for few days more and was in two minds as to send it or not. If the letter was sent to her, she might get annoyed and he might be kicked out of his job and lose his dignity or what was left of it. On the other hand he thought that it would be cowardly of him if he did not send the letter. It was better to face the consequence of his action and thus be a man as to face the outcome whether it would be good or bad

 He called on one of the friends of Sohni and managed to deliver the letter through her to Sohni and waited the reaction. He spent the following few days in a stressful mood. At last the day came when the messenger retuned with heartening news that she would see him at her home.

He wanted to present himself in a positive manner and so donned himself in a new silk shirt with langa to go with it. He put on a scarlet turban and a colorful waistcoat as to make himself presentable. He carried a small cane to give him an appearance of a refined gentleman.

 On reading his letter, Sohni was not annoyed at all but actually was pleased to receive attention and compliments of a gentleman. She thought it was right for a man to approach her first as it kept her in a dominant position – in a sort of 'upper hand' position. But who knows the workings of human heart? Once you get involved in loving someone or get attracted to a member of the opposite sex, all our logical workings of mind went out of window and the hidden workings of the passion took over and this might be happening to her.

When Karan arrived, he was shown into the drawing room to wait. Soon Sohni arrived dressed in a suit of fetching colours and when she moved about there was a whiff of scented air issuing forth from her. He found it to be seductive and when it was inhaled there was an air of overpowering surrender to his emotional self under that charm. It was wholly pleasurable sensation surrounded with the graces of her slender bodily movements. He felt that under the spell of such feminine charm he had no chance of escape and likely to yield to any pressure directed by that angel in disguise. She sat in a chair and gathered her wits about and waited for him to break the ice and bring forth his reasons for seeing her.

'Do not be afraid, I will carry all your order to full and satisfy all your desires' he nearly blurted out.

She observed him, sitting awkwardly in a chair opposite her and observed that there was a lot of grace about him and that he was not like a highly masculinised macho man full of boorishness. On the contrary his eyed betrayed softness and there was a sort of feminine receptivity about him. She thought he had plenty of sensual appeal about him.

Her beauty became overpowering and even stifling to him. Her smile would go down and pierce his heart and her image would lay there forever under his skin, like a statue of some tyrannical god. Beauty was a double- edged sword, wounding and gratifying at the same time. It gave blood to bloodless but those with enough blood had the misfortune of having their blood drained away by some invisible hands.

Anyhow what sort of spell he was under and what was he to do now? Leaving it alone or abandoning it was as bad as accepting its power over him. He was going to take his chance, whatever the cost may be.

In The Days of Love

'What have you in your mind?' Sohni asked

'I am sorry to say but your attitude towards me has changed?'

'In what way?'

'It used to be warm and friendly but now it is sort of indifferent and cold.'

'You are wrong, you are mistaken about a girl's attitude.'

'Do you hate me?'

'No I do not think so.'

'Since I saw you, I cannot get you out of my mind. I may be foolish but that is how I feel. I cannot survive in that cold empty universe. I need somebody to have regard for me.'

'What else?' heartened, Sohni teased.

'And someone to care for me.' He repeated himself

'I am here to care for, are you there to care for me?'

'Look into my heart, you are the only person residing there. Whatever you may call it- friendship or love or whatever other names you may care to call it.' Karan declared his feelings with heavy voice.

He bent down to the floor in a sort of begging position and tried to get hold of her hand and which she withdrew. Under the overwhelming emotions, he lost all his logic and fear and caught hold of her hand again in a firm grip and would not let go and this time she did not withdrew it but blushed deeply as it was the first time a man had touched her so deeply. She was trembling and her heart was racing fast within her bosom with tremendous excitement and happiness. A warmth ran through her body and her body began to perspire and a gush of blood advanced to her temples which made her ill at ease and her legs gave away. She lowered herself into the chair, with Karan still holding her hand and kissing it with his warm lips. Tears flowed from his eyes and she felt those drops of warm liquid dripping on her hands and warming it.

To take a respite from that emotional avalanche she tried to push him away but he would not let her move away .He embraced her legs into a tight grip and begged her not to abandon him. She had never seen a man in so much emotions turmoil and in such pitiable condition and she felt a wave of tenderness for that man.

He began to kiss her covered legs and went down all the way to her bare feet and began to kiss these with a torrent of emotions. She could not stand anymore and lifted him up in her arms and entangled herself around him. He had already lifted himself into a standing position eye to eye and both were locked into an embarrassing sort of physical closeness .He tightened his embrace and put his head over her shoulder still crying and with his plentiful tears staining her blouse.

In her heart of hearts Sohni was delighted with that encounter. A wave of happiness came over her and she felt like flying out of window into the calm blue sky. She wanted to return her emotions and embraced him tenderly but managed to keep some control over herself and her behaviour.

Suddenly she felt herself to be ill or ill at ease due to some undisclosed sickness. A kind of feverish excitement was going to give her a heartache and sleepless nights to follow but now she thought that she was on the verge of discovering the cause for her malady. It was so simple and at the same time so complicated. She found herself living and alive in the presence of Karan. While her imagination saturated with love for him was tortuous, but at the same time therapeutic and she wanted to live close to him forever and thus might find the cure for all her maladies.

So it was love that was her malady and a cure for it was more love, she needed love of a man and to receive plenty of it from that man. How complex were the emotions of her adulthood! One moment you were going out of your mind and a season in hell and now that action of loving brought her back into the paradise. But love did not always stay on the same intense level and like life it was changeable with its sunshine and shadows. Love was half torture and half happiness and when you were happy, you were elated and felt like flying across the rainbows of multi hues and the universe suddenly expanded to accommodate all your reveries. On the other hand when the person you love was out of sight, you got into all sort of troubles and worries. So love was an addiction, a trap but a trap of delicious taste, hopes and excitement.

 She knew that she was going to have plenty of sleepless nights and under the transportation of love reveries, she would still be tossing in her bed even at midnight hours. She had no prior experience of such matters and had to learn it in hard way on her own. Her only consolation was that he was in the same position and any embarrassment indulged by the lovers would not be so humiliating and that each one would have to learn and forget any blunders committed during their acts. For the time being it was just delicious to get locked in each other's arms but first they had to find a way to indulge in those acts, though it would be difficult to initiate it, somewhere hidden from the public gaze.

In such act they did indulge but found it initially hard going due to their non-experience in such matters .Each one was afraid that they would embarrass or annoy their partner, either through blunder or some 'considered rudeness' but when the moment came their deep emotions took over and pushed them involuntary to fall for each other's physically . Whence it was done, the passions took over as they sought each other's lips. It was funny and embarrassing as their noses became an obstacle when trying to kiss and they had to find a way around it.

Their first kiss was short but to them earth shattering and mind blowing - shock of a new experience with soul enhancing effect. They soon recovered and surrendered to it wholly. The second kiss was of more of an emotional recovery through acquired poise. It enabled them to explore the hidden depths of their spirits. Mingling with sweet juices of loving and caring, their tongues needed to explore those intricacies of spiritual and physical act. A great peace and satisfaction descended over their minds and in their bodies they felt secure as if being embraced by greater forces of the universe, acting through their bodies. It was a moment of great discovery where time lost its normal flow and life and death became one under the heat of emotions. They felt that they could die in each other's arms and even if they had died at that moment, it would not have mattered. Such was the miraculous power of love, which they just tasted.

It was beyond logic and they were venturing in a land of super-logic. Things took a new role and propelled them into a new dimension of being and if they were brave enough to let go, they might soon find themselves in an unknown land. A land without any pathways and where they had to create a new path beyond logical and could possibly find riches of unknown origins. It was happening to those souls and it would take ages comprehend it.

That experience affected them greatly and a new attraction sprang forth- for fusing their souls into a new entity. A transformation took place and it seemed that the world had changed for better. But they soon realized that they would have to climb down from those dizzy heights to mundane day today realities when they had to change themselves to thus accommodate those romantic longings with it. It did not matter as long as they had co presence of each other close by. They began to prying people of the village.

Sohni belonged to a rich family and her father owned a great deal of land .He was a prominent citizen and a pillar of the society and everybody expected an exemplary and ethical behaviour from him and his family. It was a stringent standard to be followed by other folks. Any deviation from that code of behaviour was bound to be damaging to the family. Moral laxity was bound to affect their social status in a conservative society at large. He was sure that her beloved daughter would preserve the traditions and values. He was sure that one day she would marry a suitable man chosen by her father in an arranged marriage set up and that would be celebrated with great pomp and circumstance. He could not envisage to the contrary and was sure enough of her daughter's loyalties to him and to the family and to the society's code of behaviour and the traditions.

*

The room was on the third floor, overlooking the river. It was an enchanting view of the river, slowly meandering on its way to the unknown seas.

But at low tide, the banks became wider with shingles and blackish sand showing in, with some littered stuff, debris and deposits of various objects thrown in by the people, prisoners of throw away society. Most horrifying being the brown bottles of various shapes and sizes with dull garish colours, which became adept in the art of floating and somehow remaining at their location, however strong the tide, may be.

They had made their floating spots as their permanent home unless removed by eye sore noticing river authorities.

It was completely different at high tide when all the man made horrors and ugly shingles were completely covered with slate blue wavy sheet of water and then the panorama advanced on the verge of near dazzle. It was so especially on the onset of evening when the whole place got lit up with the brush strokes of illuminated shades, yellow reflection from the tall houses built on the banks.

For the two people inside the flat, the view had its own reality giving it a sense of wider horizons and a mind-expanding stimulation, which as would seen later be a very useful ingredient in the art of loving.

Their presence to near each other induced a strange magic in the surroundings and they were affected by that overwhelming atmosphere of sensuality and love. A sensuality more lasting and concrete than mere indulgence in exhausting their sexual passions through sexual discharges and thus getting rid of that very passion which incorporated a taste for life in the first place. The secret behind it was indefinable. A wave of tenderness came over his heart and his arms began to ache for the enclosure, around Sohni's elegant body and he proceeded towards her, which she did not resist. It was beyond her rational mind as not to resist, a feeling of strong urgency to surrender herself to the power of love and longing. A new taste for the life was born in her heart, which seemed to lift her out of her body, into milliard dimensions of zigzagging physicality.

He touched her hand which she did not withdrew, cupped his hand over her hand and lifted it up, to the level of his lips and slowly kissed it. He ran his soft kisses on the entire length of her arm and pulled her towards him in a tight embrace and put his cheek against her. It felt cold but began to warm under the kisses of his warm lips. He lifted both her hands and put it on his cheeks. Her hands spread out and embraced him around her neck and then shoulders and both sought the refuge of their mouths. Soon their lips met and both were lost in a dazzle of trance. They drank from each other's mouth, which tasted sweet and it intensified the fire of passions in their bodies.

They were walking by the sea, holding each other, arm in arm and the sand below their feet was soft, warm and springy. As they walked they pressed their hands tighter for better communications and the corpuscles in their blood raced around their e bodies giving it a sense of well-being and an anticipation of new things to come.

The sky became intense blue and the water more translucent, so clear that you could see the bottom of the sea by the shore where multicoloured fishes were swimming with their mouths and noses responding to the rhythms of their breathing. All these things had an effect and their senses became acuter reflecting all the wavelengths of r instincts and sensibilities.

He looked into her eyes and deep channel of light henceforth issued, and he felt that if not careful he could drown into those depths. It began to expand perhaps to the end of galaxy and through which he could travel. The channel contained so many dimensions of emotions, of love and intimacy and at the same time it ushered in something else- a dimension of strangeness, which he wanted to explore but was fearful that if he went too far, he might reach the a point of no return, from which it would be difficult to come to his present point of departure. In order to retain that position, he tightened his grip around the body of his beloved and tears of high emotions began to flow out of his eyes.

A realization came to him that as beyond the nature was the super nature and as beyond love there might be super love, which dispensed altogether with the laws of our ordinary consciousness. His brain could not make any sense of it and had to bring in a mode of super consciousness to comprehend it all and still it was a pathless country through which one had to find one's own

*

Now he was hooked to love and wanted her around him all the time. Was it simple infatuation? He pondered about it. If another girl came along with the same beauty and charm, would he be able to desert Sohni and go for her? And after hard soul searching the answer in all his honesty was 'No'. It happened sometime that there was a love at first sight and it had happened to him and he had become the victim of it. How could it have happened- there was no denying that it was there and he was stuck with it.

In the silence of the night, Karan contemplated on his life and on his new found love for Sohni. He was sitting on a boulder in the wilderness and in his deep contemplative state he reached the land of reveries. Within deep depths he found a resonance for some contemplation of grandeur, a sunlit land resonating with all sort of riches-riches not of material sensations but some inner riches hiding in the nooks and corners of his mind and soon they began to pour out like torrents breaking the containments of his discriminatory mind. They began to envelope the landscape around him and soon the demarcation between the inner and outer realities gone. Soon he felt her presence nearby and as he began to touch it with his mind and felt that the whole space was saturated with that presence.

He realized that those emotions had given him a glimpse into some visionary reality and when he came out of that heightened emotional mood and he could not face that prospect as when he would be back into that ordinary reality of barren thinking ushered in by people's pressure that had no concern with such moments. Soon he would be in the land of those human values with utilitarian ends but was glad to have a glimpse of that non ordinary reality. He was glad and thankful to Sohni for bringing a temporary respite into his troubled mind. How did it happen? He could not put his finger on it.

An avalanche of poetical musing overwhelmed him and expressed itself in words of that un-expressible reality.

LADY OF NOURISHMENT

Lady of nourishment
Hidden of excess
Sacred of power
Ruler of distinct.

Seven scorpions galling
Plotting their revenge
Dreaded of poisons
Stings in firmaments.

Moulder of mountains
Creator of the maze
Tuner of the silence
Carver of the embrace.

Lady of nourishments
Ruler of the distinct
Server of enchantment
Breather of incense.

After years of wilderness, he realized that he had come closer to a mode where he might find emotional support and might be more-something unknown that was beyond reach of mind. For a logical person it was just hocus pocus of fancies without any foundations in the material realm. They called it a 'poetical fancy 'and to which the 'poetical' in him replied 'what you call fancy is not fanciful at all but an imagination of first order without which life will lose its significance.'

Imagination was an essential part of human thinking and acting. One imagined future and worked towards it, it allowed one to move forward and backward at the juncture of memories. Strangely there could be a past as well as future in memories and imagination gave it a shape. It was a phenomenology of human thinking and he could not get away from it. One might even imagine that in most of animal kingdom there might not be real imagination at work and so the creatures lived only in the present. Without any imagination about their future, the animals might live without any awareness of death, the fear of which took the sail out of human hopes. Living always in the present had its own advantages but a sensitive man could not reconcile himself to such a mode of insensibility.

If you look closely, lot of human endeaviour was linked to search for human happiness, for the present and future for which we plan unconsciously- money making, finding love, future welfare of one's children etc. Our instinct for death had resulted in all sorts of enterprises. It was to find some sort of meaning either in our lives or for consideration of one's standing in the society however trivial this notion might be.

And what about depth psychology of male and female forces. Metaphysical concepts and a search for higher form of human reality- visionaries had been indulging in defining such forces. Theses might consist of some sort of therapeutic effects on our physical and emotional bodies and it was directly related to our experiences, of interaction of such dual forces. According to certain Indian religious metaphysics, nothing was inert, mechanically driven or unrelated to life of our universe. Even the constituents of atom had their counterpart in male/female forces, for instance electron was designated as of female orientation and when their circulatory movement towards its male counterpart was affected, burst of energy of life forces issued. Consequently the whole basis of material ,emotional and metaphysical reality had it basis in male and female energies.

 The poetical mind instinctively felt all that instinctively present, forms in notion of a 'muse'. To ordinary thinking it was just nothing - fanciful notion but to a poetical mind it had a concrete reality. Even in medieval mind it was a concrete notion where the knights paid homage to their ladies and did heroic things for the sake of their muses. Search for such' muse's love 'changed the course of few lives, having inspired an artistic revolution for spiritual and higher aims. Even in modern times such notion of a 'muse' still persisted.

He was indebted to Sohni, for such thoughts:

LADY OF MY DREAMS

Moon colored
Raven haired
Inaccessible
Like a distant shore.

Dwelling here
Closer to the heart

A reason a dream
Undefined yet real.

Moon colored pebbles
Shining among plains
A cluster
Deeply driven
Etched like a wound
A rose or a moan
Or a crimson scar
A luminosity
Or a distant spark.

Lady of my heart
Moon colored
Raven haired
Inaccessible
Like a distant star.

Chapter Six

Sohni's father Jaswant was a nice upright gentleman who loved his children very much and especially Sohni who happened to be his favourite daughter. People around the village told him again and again that he would spoil her with too much loving and caring but he ignored these warnings as something without foundation.

Jaswant had an elder brother who lived about fifty miles away where he too had a family and owned a large tract of land. His name being Balwant. He too was very fond of her niece and whenever he visited them, he brought lots of presents both for his nephew and niece. Sohni too was fond of her uncle. One day it was announced that her uncle would be coming soon to meet the family. Normally she would have been overjoyed to see him and spend all her time with him but this time she was not so enthusiastic. It looked, as due to her acquaintance with Karan, she wanted to spend more time with him.

Soon the uncle duly arrived with lots of present. He had not visited them since two years and an impression of her as being still a child and thus brought suitable present for that age. Normally Sohni would be at the doorstep of the house to greet him but this time there was no one to receive and he went straight to the inner courtyard where his brother was busy doing some jobs connected with farming business. He was busy in operating the hand machine using it to make fodder for the animals. He was operating a large wheel manually and the blade attached to it was shredding the green stalks inserted into feeder and the shredded pieces coming out at the other end from under the blade, which the animals could easily manage to eat.

The uncle enquired about Sohni and he was told that she was out supervising workers in the fields and specially a new cowherd who had recently joined them, to look after the animals. She was engaged in supervising and training this new man and hence could not be at home to receive her uncle.

It was late in the evening when she returned home and seemed glad to see her uncle. She had grown up and turned into a handsome young woman and the uncle could hardly recognize her. When he saw her last time she was a merely a child and now how she had grown! Her shining beauty was sufficient enough to turn any man's head and who could resist her or take their eyes of her. Furthermore her beauty had that quality which was hard to define verbally but so overpowering as to be felt instinctively.

Sohni practically shone with happiness and well-being.

'How are you my daughter?' enquired the uncle

'I am very well.' Replied Sohni beaming.

'You looked very happy.'

'Yes I am very happy and feel at the top of the world.'

'It looks that you have found a treasure?'

'Yes it is a sort of treasure.'

'Let me guess. It is either that you have found a pot of gold or a handsome man to flirt with.' Said the uncle jokingly.

He could see a streak of blush blossoming across her face.

'I hope that you have found a rich handsome man as your future partner' Uncle teased her.

'I did not say anything about it. Only thing I can say is that things are running very well now.' Replied Sohni suppressing her embarrassment.

'Has he found anything about my relationship with Karan?' thought she, half in fright as she knew that he or her family would not approve of Karan as he was now a penniless and a mere cowherd in their service. In that society it is scandalous to think of a pretty daughter of a rich man marrying a penniless labourer.

Uncle was not much concerned with her bashful attitude and did not suspect anything out of usual. It was the normal thing with the young girls at the outset of that age- an awakening to adulthood and sexuality. The only thing that an adult could do was to give advice and guidance to teens - teens on the threshold of adulthood.

As the uncle was very fond of her ever since her birth, he was always thinking about her future in earnest and was sure that her future would conform to the normal social code of the society and in her case, the paramount was respectability. He had no interest in exploring hidden or forbidden avenues of human behaviour. He was brought up in a traditional stalwart household, always guided by his parents and other elders.

When he started his primary education and entered the school at the age of six, he had to conform to everything that society and tradition demanded. In reality he disliked the teachers and the way he was taught. He thought that most of the teachers were boorish and cruel and made use of their authority ruling over little children. He thought that they acted like bullies. The use of corporal punishment was widespread and teachers would use it on any pretext and strictly kept to the motto ' spare the rod and spoil the child' and if any child went out of the normal way to show any trace of individuality, he became an anathema to the teacher. He must be punished and goaded that way, society was going to fall apart.

Like all other liberal young men who started their lives with idealistic aims, he also started likewise and followed up such path with high hopes of 'changing the world' but as usually it did not last long and the world changed him. Each adult had to follow the traditional course of growing up- firstly getting married via an arranged marriage instituted by the parents and most parents did look for a girl who would bring in a huge amount of dowry. Unless the bridegroom objected and fought his corner, the appearance and beauty of the bride was of secondary importance. As long the bride was of healthy constitution to bear children and provided with lavish dowry, all was well.

It was hard to go against that current of 'normality' and eventually everybody fell a prey to that conception and the exceptional few who followed ' rebellious' paths did not last long and soon joined the herd. Such was the mental state of her uncle. He had profited from such ventures as two of his sons married in rich families and with plenty of dowry loots coming in and hence he was well off and became a respectable pillar of the society. He wanted others to follow likewise.

*

The secret love lives of Sohni and Karan took a more passionate route and on the pretext of work they were meeting almost everyday. She told her parents that Karan needed a lot of supervision, to do his job properly as a cowherd. Their usual rendezvous was in some open space set within a field full of fresh grass on which the animals could graze. She brought him many selected hand cooked meals of which he was very fond off. Since his father died he had never been treated so nicely and for which he felt indebted to her .She had picked him up from gutter and placed him on a pedestal of love and respect.

As far as Sohni was concerned she received a sort of boost to her own life too. She was moving in a new territory full of love and romance and as they say love had given her wings and she felt like flying into open spaces without her feet touching the ground. She felt feverish with all that heady excitement and was acquiring new experiences and new worlds. Reveries of love were repeating themselves in her mind and were going around and around in her head and which even kept her from sleeping a full night's sleep. In that sort of dedication, she was alive only when she was with him. She could never have envisaged that her life would take that sort of turn. She was really surprised by herself and to find that she had so much romance in her soul and so much love to give.

Hand in hand they were in the wilderness where against some rocky backdrop, there was an expanse of woods through which they used to take a stroll. The subtlety of their emotions had made them sensitive to the enchantment of the surroundings and felt that they were moving through some rich territory full of novel experiences. They identify themselves with it and felt that they were the forest, they were the leaves and they were the wind gently blowing through the rustling leaves .The whole universe was coming to touch them making their senses acutely sensitive and they could respond even to the slight variation of its moods and motions. To take some relief from that strong emotional pressure, his arms extended and gently sought the contours of her body and as the hand went around her waist to pull her closer, w the other hand gripped her waist even tighter. They sat down to relish those moments.

He slowly lifted her into his lap from the ground and they became entwined like two fragile vines. The heat and energy oozing from their body was overwhelming and a warm wave rose and enveloped their brains seeking even closer contacts of souls. Amid sighs and moans they sought the refuge of their lips. The gentle touch of four lips intensified the fire within and in order to quench this, they sought the coolness of their mouths and tongues and soon they were drinking from each other's mouth. Each one was probing deeper and deeper into each other, the moistness of their mouths mingled and they drank heartily from it. It was a sweet and invigorating wine, which gave them an intense taste of life.

They moved on and walked hand in hand towards distant hills. It was evening and the long rays of the sun were colouring the landscape with various shades of orange and yellow. The air was cool and balmy and there was a silence around them providing them with spaces to project their emotions- of mutual caring and love and they felt that these rebounded, coming back as blessings from some divine. They could envisage newfound enthusiasm in the skies above covered with golden fleecy clouds- the gentle breezes, the canopy of leaves, the cries of some solitary bird and occasional chirping of cicadas and that they found amiable and conducive to their bright high romance. They have entered those dimensions of universe which cater for such romantic interludes and where things take on new realities and which are barred to day to day mundane routines.

Here was the imagination in all its glory, an imagination in whose furnace all the realities were melted and in crucible of passion to produce diamonds of translucent colours molded to like distant stars. The trouble was that very few could reach that stage of realty. It took a lot of courage and intelligence to explore such vistas. When love was born it was simply in all its imperfections and perfections and nobody could dare to define it or gave it a single direction. The trouble with our logical faculty being it always tried to dominate other faculties of mind as this chief controller and considered itself a supremo to dominate others. Most people accepted this as a matter of logical facts. Armed with this pseudo scientific platitudes and they never understood that an emotional intelligence or super logic were equally valid.

And how could you define love. It was an experience and not logical phenomena, it was a priori and logic came afterwards. How could you define a green colour to a person who was born blind? To define a thing was to make a verbal substitute in its place and which had little or nothing to do with the original experience and hence a complete falsity. The egoist faculty of human mind wanted a total dominance over emotions but love would never yield to such a dominance. The best thing for lovers was to acknowledge the true phenomenology of love and experience it in all its richness. In order to love truly, one had to be brave to accept mutual differences and variety of human feelings and thus come to a 'world of values', which constituted the human psyche. To love a person was to create a world of values, however idealistic these might be and acting thus to become a part of those values. .

*

They say that everybody loves the lovers but truth is far from it. As a matter of fact when people see lovers romancing about amid frolics, it bread jealousy and lead to hatred for those who had someone to love and which most people lacked. The truth could be that everyone or almost everyone hated lovers.

As 'secret' meetings of Karan and Sohni became more and more open, people began to see them in public more often walking close to each other or sitting together holding hands and so the tongues started wagging.

'Have you seen their behaviour, they have no shame.'

'A single girl meeting a single man in front of strangers, it is disgusting!'

'What are the girl's parents doing? Are they blind to the things going on in the village?'

'It should be stopped immediately, they are corrupting our children.'

And so on.

In a conservative society bound by traditions and rules of behaviour, it was outrageous that single girl should have a relationship with a man outside the marriage and moreover it was unthinkable that the daughter of a rich farmer should cahoot with a poor penniless man who happened to be a cowherd and was the world coming to an end? It was beyond the mental capacity of traditionally bound villagers without any spark of originality

Soon it became a favourite past-time among the women folks, delighting in gossip and backbiting, discussing that hot topic of the day with all its scandalous undertones. Most farmers' wives delighted in such back biting pastime.

Soon these gossips went beyond their own village and spread beyond its confines to the wider vicinity ands soon came to the ears of uncle, in all its exaggerated forms. Someone told him that the couple was sleeping together most of the nights while the other indicated that he had seen them making love in the bushes. These people delighted to shock and upset the uncle to their utmost and did indeed upset him. He wanted to find out more about the relationship of the parties concerned. Being busy and living away from Sohni's village, he could not go and do the detective work himself and so called on the services of a man he could depend on. He directed him to do such detective work for him but made him sworn about the high secrecy of the project. They agreed upon the fees for the work undertaken and uncle paid half of the sum agreed and other half was to be paid after the investigations and resulted in concrete evidence or valid proofs.

The detective set to work, donned himself as a beggar and proceeded to Sohni's village. His first task was to get acquainted with her. He told the villagers that he was a poor and destitute man from a remote district, driven out on account of hunger and poverty and came to that village to seek help as he had heard about the generosity of the village folks. People pointed out to him that he should go and see Sohni as to seek help from her. She was reputed to be a champion of poor and downtrodden. He kept a watch outside her house as to her arrival and departure from the house. He noticed that she always disappeared in late morning and returned about mid afternoon and even sometime in the evenings just before the approach of the dark. He wanted to keep his distance from her, in case she spotted him while he was following her to spy on.

He also wanted to catch a glimpse of the inside of the house and when he saw her going out of the house, he made sure that she did not return home. He donned his beggar's garb, took his begging bowl and called at the house.

'Hey mother, hey father, a hungry beggar has arrived at your door. Help him!'

As usual nobody listened to his pleas as was the common practice among householders who were daily pestered by many beggars and vagabonds each day.

The beggar still persisted with the begging ritual.

'May God grant you plenty of sons and may Laxmi ,the goddess of wealth showers her favours on you!'

The housemaid saw it that it was a stubborn beggar and won't go away, came out and asked him what he wanted.

'Give food to a hungry beggar, dear child, may God bless you.'

'It is only mid morning, food will not be prepared before lunch, come back then.' Retorted the maid. 'Anyhow you do not look like a real beggar to me. You look like a scoundrel, a badmash.'

'Dear child, do not speak such harsh words. I am a real beggar and belong to begging class, all my forefathers and relations have been beggars too.' Said the beggar trying to impress the maid.

'But you do not look starved as you say. You look to me very well fed.'

'Do not insult the ascetics, child! Do not bring burden of sins on yourself.'

'What about yourself baba! You are bringing the burden of sins on yourself by lying.' Said the maid delighted in taking her revenge.

The beggar was afraid that if he persisted in arguing with the short, he said:

'OK child, bring some flour for the baba and he will make the chapattis himself.'

The maid brought him a handful of floor and she was glad to get rid of that scoundrel.

In The Days of Love

The beggar while conversing with the maid had plenty of time to glance through the open door and assessed that the house belonged to a prosperous and rich family.

He changed his appearance again and donned himself as a peasant from another district and who wanted to buy some fertile land in that part of the world.

He began to follow Sohni on her morning walks and soon discovered that she went straight to some grazing lands outside the village where he met a man supposedly a cowherd and talked to her, pretending to give him some instruction. Soon they disappeared holding hands into a thicket. The spy was glad that at least he had found some evidence of the relationship between the two parties under suspicion. The next thing to do was to find their hidden whereabouts and how they spent their time during their meet ups in afternoon and evenings.

He soon found out that Karan was employed by Sohni's father in the capacity of a cowherd and presumed that he would be living close by their house somewhere on the land owned by them. Firstly he had to find the location of the land owned by that family. He was afraid to make enquiries from the village folks in case he was discovered as a spy. He had to go to the village patwari, the keeper of land records and bribed him to give him the exact location of their land holdings. He searched the holdings and found a small cottage in one of the grove and kept a vigil there until he found the comings and goings of Sohni and the meetings of her with her lover Karan. He kept a diary of all these happenings for a few days and when he had sufficient evidence, he went back to her uncle and presented those and for which he was paid the rest of outstanding fees in respect of the detective work rendered.

The uncle was shocked about the goings on in his brother's house. He was sure that the family's name was going to be disgraced on account of his niece's conduct. A young girl should not have any liaison with any member of opposite sex while she was unmarried and under her father's protection. He blamed his brother who was in some way responsible for all that sorry state of affairs and considered him to be somewhat naive and lax in such matters of discipline on his family. He thought it was his duty to guide his brother in the right direction. He must go immediately to their village, investigate the whole matter and try to nip it in bud any such rumours before it got out of hand and maligned the family's name. He proceeded on his journey.

Uncle Balwant arrived at the house in an agitated state and a sour face ready to pour his pent up emotions and grievances but did not find his brother at home. He searched for him and found him in his fields directing a farm labourer on the art of vegetable cultivation as he was himself very fond of growing vegetables, good enough for sale in the markets of nearby town. Balwant urged him to stop his work immediately and come home with him as he had to discus some urgent matters with him in complete privacy.

'Has anybody died? Or something?' he said jokingly as his elder brother was prone to exaggerating things and turning them into crisis.

'It is worse than death; the reputation of whole family is at stake.'

'There cannot be anything worse than death. Calm down and I will be with you after I have finished my work with farm hands.' Jaswant told him

Balwant did not take it lightly and kept pacing up and down for an hour until the work of his brother was finished and they arrived soon at their house. He informed his brother about the scandalous rumors in the district of the love affair his niece was having with a low cowherd and which was going to affect their family's name and a great calamity was waiting to fall on the family.

Jaswant kept his calm and told his brother that nothing calamitous was going to happen and he would investigate the situation and speak to her daughter in private. Those were the usual things happen in the course of family life and everybody when young had sometime indulged in such flirtations but were put right these when advised by the parents. But Balwant was not listening to him and was still full of agitations. He could not handle the coming situation and was putting a great deal of imagination into it to exaggerate it.

Suppose the girl was ordered not to see Karan anymore and kept strictly under the family's control and suppose she refused to accept such situation and what would happen then? She might even elope with that fellow and look at the shame she would bring on all her relations and family .His brother was too innocent to know such scandalous goings on in the world. He was looking on the world through rosy tinted glasses but the world was full of evil and corruption and that was his job to direct his brother accordingly. He must see the girl himself and cross- examine her about the whole affair and whether she admitted it or not, was of no consequence, his spy had confirmed everything.

He wanted to see Sohni straight away and to convey his anger about the way she was behaving and not caring much for the family's name. He was full of rage and never expected such things from such a sweet and innocent girl. She had been her favourite niece and how she had let down her uncle so badly. With his big ego, he always considered himself as the head of the clan and like a general he had to control the family's behaviour and lead them up a honorable path, worthy of a the family's name and its social standing in the society. If she or his brother did not listen to him, he had to find an alternative way to deal with it himself.

He went back to his village and brooded over it for days and thought he found a solution at last. He had to find a suitable marriage partner for her before the things got out of hand completely.

*

He called in all the matchmakers of the district and requested them to find a suitable groom for her beloved niece. She was beautiful, clever, intelligent and would bring a lot of dowry as she belonged to a rich father. With these grand assets there would be no dearth of suitable boys and most families would be falling over each other to secure her as a bride for their sons. So it turned out to be it was and the matchmakers provided him with a list of suitable matches. He decided to take a few days off from his work and visit those suitors and their parents, to see for himself. He informed his brother that he soon would be going on a quest to find a suitable partner for her niece and would then inform him about his choice and which would be binding on him as he was his elder brother and the decision maker of the family.

The concept of arranged marriages might seem odd to an outsider but from the point of the people of the country, it was not so .In that society an arranged marriage was considered to be an act of love too, since marriage was the most important decision a person was likely to make. Breakage of marriage was considered a disaster in one's life. When you were young and fell in love for the first time with a stranger, the emotional involvement and novelty being so strong that you did not have a chance to judge it with a cool head and normally get entangled in a mazeful of false sentiments. Attractions and lifelong commitments were two different things and it was better to be left with the elders.

It was understandable that the choice of a marriage partner should be carefully thought out by those who had some experience of it and it was reasonable that the family or parents should look for certain merits in the future partner- the conduct of the future bridegroom and thus the matter should be put under close scrutiny. What was the general reputation of the groom's family? Do the women folks in that family were treated well? Was the groom well disciplined and hardworking to provide the support for the future bride? Were there many brothers and sisters of the groom, the fewer the better otherwise she might have to serve all in a subservient role to them.

Potential brides also came under scrutiny as she should be embodiment of the family's honour and pride but sadly these were not of paramount importance to groom's parents. Greed was the common vice of the most of the humanity and so the question of dowry the bride was going to bring bringing with her, outweighed everything else and became the most important issue in a sort of 'bride's-price'. The groom's parents might ask for a lot of furniture for the household, golden jewellery and beautiful expansive clothes for the in-laws and all their distant relations. All these could amount to substantial sum- a considerable burden on bride's parents. All those social ills were ignored and pushed under the carpet for sole sake of greed and respectability.

So the uncle went on a pilgrim to find a suitable match for her niece. Some of the families he visited were not up to his standards of decent behaviour. Either the boy or the parents were manner less, brutish or suffering from lack of education even though they were rich with plenty of land. Others were too greedy asking for vast amounts of dowry. One unsuitable groom was always drunk and addicted to opium and o drug taking. At last he found an honest, well to do family with a handsome looking potential groom. They did not insist on any asking amount of dowry but were pleased to have it left to the choice of bride's parents. All in all, the uncle was pleased with his work and with the choice of the groom he had made.

He went back to Sohni's house and told her father about the details of his choice regarding the prospective groom. The father did not like the goings on behind his back but as was customary he had to listen to his elder brother's advice and abide by his decision. He had to break the news to her daughter but did not have the heart to do so as he knew that it would shatter her to pieces. The uncle encouraged his brother to call Sohni in to their presence as to give her the news. The girl suspected something bad was in the offing when she was called suddenly like that in front of the elders. Her eyes were moist and she was on the point of bursting into tears.

Her father first spoke to her in a sad tone:

'Dear daughter, now you have grown up into a fine young woman and as is customary in
our society, it is our duty to find a suitable match for you.'

The girl's whole world came tumbling down and big sobs followed indicating great tortures in her soul.

'Father, I do not want to get married.' She cried in a tearful voice

'As you know, a young daughter cannot remain forever with her parents as the custom of our land demands, otherwise tongues will start wagging.'

'Let them wag. I do not care for those tongues.'

In The Days of Love

'But I have to care. I have a family to protect and care for. I cannot make other people my enemies. I have to live in this society.'

'I do not want to marry a person whom I have never seen and whom I may never love.'

The uncle saw that situation was getting out of hand and taking a turn for worse and so he intervened.

'I will select a lovely match for you and you will have all the opportunity to meet him soon and see whether you like him.' Uncle was trying to trap her into a cul- de- sac.

'But I will never be able to love him.'

'Love does not grow on the trees. You have to work hard to acquaint yourself with a person and then love will follow.'

'I cannot do that.' Sohni protested with tearful jerks in her voice.

'You are showing a lot of emotions. Is it possible that you already love someone?' uncle thought that at last he would corner her into a tight spot from where escape would be impossible for her.

'Yes, I love someone.' She said boldly

'Is it Karan? The cowherd. 'He demanded

'Yes it is.' She said with sob stifling her voice.

The uncle now turned to his brother, trying to prolong his triumph.

'Jaswant! See what you have done .By being soft and women like, you have spoilt your children. They do not have any shame in confessing such dreadful things in front of their elders.'

'Do not blame my father. He had been best of dads. He taught me to be independent minded. He had been a most loving father.' Sohni leapt into her father's defence

Her father appreciated that support from her daughter but thought too that her choice was made under infatuation, of the youth's very first experience of love.

'But dear daughter! You cannot marry a cowherd who had no future prospects. You have been brought up in luxury and he will not be able to support you in your life.'

'I will better die than to marry someone else.' Sohni went out of the room with tearful face screaming.

Breaking up a loving relationship was never easy for anyone and it not only broke up her confidence, made her feel despondent and shattered her spirits but also made it hard to trust any elders of her family and specially her uncle. It is one of the most difficult things for her to manage a heartbreak and to recover from it was neigh impossible as it was her first love affair.

 In her arranged marriage she could envisage a break up of her marriage with her future husband as there were no prospect of any mutual love and she felt that her marriage would soon be on the rock but a love affair without commitment was to her more reliable and lasting relationship. All her life she had been searching for someone special who could make her life complete and worthwhile and suddenly it had come to her so to say fallen from the sky. But now it looked like that her real life had been snatched from her. It had a melancholy tinge full of sadness and dark forebodings and she felt like that she would be going to leave a part of herself with Karan. She was just an empty shell without any soul.

It did not matter to her whether that her relationship had always been blissful and the lovers like her who could love truly were not bothered about their happiness all the time but and even a little bit of unhappiness was not a bad deal. The prime aim was to love a person truly and thus live a life of emotional depth. She had instinctively found that out.

Chapter Seven

The atmosphere in Sohni's household became sour and all the members of her household found it suffocating. All the communications seized and people shut themselves within themselves and it seemed that all the intimacy and the love between them had gone. They were surprised with such sudden change in their behaviour, all due the proposed arranged marriage of Sohni.

Would anyone dared to change the things as they were?

Her father was under such strain and would have liked to bring back some harmony in the bitterly divided household but could not find any solution to resolve the conflict. He could not allow her daughter to marry Karan and who was a penniless cowherd in his employment as a servant. In case impossible happened how could that lad be able to support her daughter for the rest of life? When even he could not support himself sufficiently in his life.

There were questions upon question but all were without any answers. Sohni had shut herself in her room and would not come out or eat properly and father could not bear her beloved daughter in such a pitiable condition. His heart was simply breaking but he could see that any positive action coming through to get them out of their grief. He wanted to help her and to see that pretty smile on her daughter's face again. But how could he do that?

Suppose against all improbabilities, she was allowed the marry Karan, where they would go and live for the rest of their lives? He had been driven out of his ancestral home and his brothers would not even allow him back to live there and anyhow they go and live in that filthy hovel of a hut which he assigned to Karan as his living quarters. He simply would be a butt of everybody in the village and would not be able to show his face to anyone outside his house. So there was no practical solution to his predicaments.

 Sohni did not want to see any members of her family and kept herself inside, behind a locked door and it was difficult for her father to have a direct talk with her. He was feeling guilty himself and wanted to show that grief at least to his daughter. One morning he knocked at her door but there was no answer, he kept repeating the knocks as he knew she was inside. At last she answered him stating she did not want to see any one, as she was not feeling well. After many a pleadings from him, she slowly opened the door and when father went inside and was so grieved to see her disheveled appearance.

'How are you daughter? I missed you terribly for the last few days.' He broke the ice

'I am sort of Ok.' She replied concealing all her grief.

'Are you angry with me?'

There was no reply as she tried to turn her face away from him.

'Are you angry with me?' he repeated, to keep the conversation going.

'Yes.'

'But why?'

'You know that.'

'But I did not intend to do any harm to you.'

'You have already done it.'

'But I had no choice.'

'Every body has a choice, if they have got a will.'

'Be fair. I am bound by rules and I live in a society which imposes its social conventions on me.'

'Rules are there to be broken. All you need is some courage.' Sohni spoke her mind.

'You are young, without any experiences of the world at large. I have obligations to all.
To society and to my kith and kin. What sort of courage are you demanding?' he said in all his sincerity.

'I do not want to marry anyone else except Karan.'

'I have nothing against him as a person but I cannot see any future prospects in his case. Be realistic, he is penniless and will not able to support you.'

'We can work as day labourers or in the farm.'

'You are not used to such life and he is unstable and unable to do anything better than cattle grazing. Be sensible nobody will employee the daughter of well known farmer in a menial job, and you will never be able to perform hard physical work, who had been brought up in luxury.'

'We will go to his brothers and beg for his inheritance.'

'What sort of inheritance will he be asking from his brothers?'

'Some land for farming.' Sohni replied

In The Days of Love

'As I gather, the brothers have already divided the land and property left by their father
and have legalized the transfer in their respective names. If he insists he can have an acre of barren land and which is not good for any crop yield.'

She realized that all her plans were only speculations and nothing concrete would come out of it. Still her love for Karan persuaded her to hope against the hope that something good would come out of it.

Her father gave her a pitiable look and she realized there was not a chink of light in the dark land of her relationship. The emotional pressure began to build up inside her and she burst into tears. Pangs of grief came over him and he took her daughter in his arms. She became more emotional and streams of tears ran down her cheeks onto her father's shoulder. Both clung to each other to escape from that avalanche of heartbreak and pain.

That overwhelming grief had blunted their rationality and a communication of silence issued.

Driven more by emotions than rationality Sohni whispered

'Father, understand that I cannot live without his love and if contrary happens, I will kill myself.'

'Do not say such foolish things. Don't you have any feelings for your unfortunate father who will not be able to bear such a jolt? Do you want to kill your father too?'

'I will never do anything to hurt my father. You were always a good father to me.'

'So pity me as a daughter will do for her unfortunate father. I know that I am breaking your heart but no other way is open to me. You must marry the man your uncle has chosen for you.'

Sohni could not bear all burden of anguish anymore and ran away to her room, threw herself on the bed and cried her heart out.

*

In most people's life, birth and marriage are the biggest occasions for celebration and so it was with her father, Jaswant. He had put all his heart in the marriage of her beloved daughter and though would not be joyous occasion as he hoped for but still he was determined to carry it through and make it a great success. He and his family set to work, nearly two months before the marriage was due. Why such a gap for preparations?

 Preparations for the marriage were a time consuming, laborious and complicated business and which involved varieties of chores to be arranged and lot of people to be contracted. People not only from lay backgrounds but people from the professional trades were required. Take for instance the matter involving aspect of the dowry system where all the burden was carried by the bride's family and where bride's parents could even go bankrupt paying the price of that dowry demanded by the groom's parents. The higher the caste you belonged to, the greater would be their expectations and there should not be a margin for an error. If the groom's people thought that the bride did not bring in the expected dowry, she was liable to be maligned and reminded for the rest of her married life. It would be an excuse to undermine her status by the mother in law who would use any hurtful and abusive language at any small occasion, to remind her that she came from a poor bankrupt family and she should think herself lucky for marrying a prince like her son.

In The Days of Love

The girl was supposed to be immune against such scolding and abuses and if unfortunately, out of anger retaliated by answering back, the mother in law would instigate a hellish atmosphere in the house. She was even liable to cause physical abuse to bride by herself or through persuasion of other male members of the household resulting in some shameful physical punishments. Some mother in laws had gone so far as torching the brides to death by sprinkling kerosene oil on her and pretending that she committed suicide herself.

In the light of above, bride's parents had to make sure that the preparations of the dowry accumulations and for hosting the marriage party were immaculate. One item of the dowry consisted in the preparations of the gifts, especially clothing and dresses for the entire groom's family and their relatives however distant they might be.

Professional tailors were contracted and would bring in all their sewing machine and professional gears to set up a temporary work area in the bride's house. Here they would be consulted and supervised for all the dress making. The first step was to buy yards and yards of clothes from which dresses were to be made, by the master tailors. There were no clothing shops in the village and so they had to go out to the nearest big town to buy it. Sohni's father accompanied other female members along with the master tailor and they were to go to town to buy all the goods, which in itself was a big undertaking, taking into account the prevalent fashions-colour, shades, patterns of the cloth.

The cloth merchant's shops were of decorative nature and inviting with rolls of various clothes arranged in neat niches along the breadth and height of the shops. The best arrangements to view variety of textiles were to sit on the cushioned floor where you could see and touch different fabrics. Once you ask for a display of certain kind, the proprietors would throw yards of unrolled materials in front of you for your inspection. Soon you were overwhelmed with abundance of choices. The trick was to make a mental note of your choice quickly as the textiles were unrolled otherwise it was near impossible to choose one, amid those sumptuous varieties.

Such a big amount of textiles were to be bought and it was going to take at least three days of bargaining and selection. Each one put forward arguments in favour of their own choice and then the arguments and discussions ensued and this could have gone on endlessly but final choice had to be made which was left to master tailor, in case if the discussions did not result in mutual agreement.

Clothes had to be chosen and designed for various men, women and children of all the groom's family plus their relations. The situation was not so bad about men and children but it was a different proposition as far women of the family were concerned who tend to be fussy and critical about the readymade garments and certainly they were going to get fussy as they received the marriage gifts from their in laws. The choice for the men was relatively simple- Shirt, long kurta, trousers, jackets, achkans or long tunics with suitable turbans to match the colour of their garments.

Easy ideas could not be applied to clothes for women. First difficulty being as to the size of the females concerned and secondly their colour preferences. Half of it was solved by actual observation. An apprentice tailor was dispatched to the village and who happened to have a friend living in that same village and over the number of the days he observed the perspective clients and reported his findings back. He found that majority of women and especially young ones were of medium height and built and which was a great relief to all the tailors preparing in preparing the dresses.

So the majority of the clothes were prepared to be of medium size measurements except few, whose structures were to be estimated as to the size and shape. It was impossible to please everyone and so a chance was taken. As a matter of fact the tailor promised to do minor alteration without charging the people involved and the cost was to be borne by the bride's family. In order to cover the suitability for all weathers, half the garments were woolen and the other half would be made in cotton material .It was a great relief to the family to have at least solved this thorny question of the gift of dresses to be given as a part of dowry.

 Ladies clothes consisted of saris, salwar kamiz with appropriate head covering scarves
of suitable colours and materials..

*

The people of that land had spent time and energy for centuries, in the creation of ornaments and decoration for the human body and especially for the female form. The human spirit craves for the intangible to be made into tangible and invisible to be made into visible, such as from the grounds of our existence Thus aesthetic desires came into being and which led to variety of inventions and experimentations. Arts and crafts bloomed to give vent to these desires an expressions of human personality in varieties of ways.

 Desire inherent in female psyche for enhancement of sensual appeal of its body had always been present and took different forms of inventions in accordance with the fashion prevalent in each age and also in accordance with spiritual and socio-economics environments. It was specially so with the Indian mode of thinking which took notice of all the variations of expressing of the spiritual aspirations into their physical counterparts.

Indeed rarely was a traditional ornament designed simply to be decorative or somehow devoid of inherent meaning or symbolic value. The jewellery acted as a metaphorical language, which could be communicated direct from the wearer to the viewer.
Such ornamentation delved into the vast reserve of symbolically significant forms and images stored over ages by the human intellect and its activity. The jewellery was created from such images, some obvious, some subtle and some from images whose origin had been forgotten in the annals of dark past.

Complementary to such thought was the conventional view where the graceful form of a female was said to epitomize the ideal beauty hidden in some mystical higher sense. Thus befittingly each part of feminine physique including head, torso, arms, legs, hands and feet was considered to be carrying a life force of their own. Each part had to be given its due by enhancement and dedication of appropriate ornamentation in an ingenious ways The subtle idea being that only things covered with ornamentation are beautiful as they draw the attention of the viewer and thus set up a chain of association in their minds.

This poetry of the body must overflow with rhetorical ornaments- alamkaraa, which decorate or adorn, to justify its inner spirit. It was analogous to a sort of musical composition, a poetry of sensuality and of these women were such natural carriers. Ornamentation not only served to please the eye of the beholder but also fulfilled an auspicious aim, an impulse from deep sensibility to mark an occasion for living with fruitful symbols. Designs and marks were made to evoke good fortune and to seek protection from the evil forces of the world.

In The Days of Love

The thinkers translated the abstract written philosophy of the ancient texts into the concrete reality of everyday life and canonized the adornments of the female form into sixteen different categories or the Solah Shingar, covering the entire female body from toe to head. The choice of sixteen numbers corresponded to the sixteen phases of the moon and which in turn symbolized with a woman's menstrual cycle and in a deep sense indicated that even the biological functions of the body had their roots in the spiritual realm.

First priority for buying the jewellery was for the sake of bride as she would be judged primary by the number of gold ornaments she was wearing brought in from her parents house. The bangles were important and as theses were made of gold, of weighty cast costing much in monetary form. This had a twofold purpose, one being to impress in-laws and other as a hedge against any possible future hard times. Women's jewellery was considered to be a sort of financial insurance against bad times. Gold never lost its value even in unstable political times and in which the paper money could have been devalued. Consequently married women had a special attachment to their golden ornaments and guarded it with all their lives.

Next in the list were the necklaces or haars, which could be as valuable as the bangles as they incorporate solid gold structures. Beside the gold some of these could be of cheaper format such as of glass beads or of other precious stones. These were not so costly and so could be parted as gifts for women folks of groom's household. Such clever designs and arrangements of colour combinations in precious stone were much appreciated all around.

Nath or the nose ornament was a circular ring inserted through a pierced nose. The nose was first believed to exclusively concerned with smell but later was established to be connected with emotional responsivity also. In occultist circles it was considered to be part of sixth sense. Anyhow it increased the sensual appeal of the bride for the groom to be. The land's aesthetic sensibilities befittingly adorned the female nose with an inspired ornament, which highlighted its amorous appeal. Indeed amongst many jewels with which the woman adorned herself, the nose ornament was perhaps the most seductive. Theses ornaments took on variety of shapes ranging from tiny jeweled studs resting on the curve of the nostrils, to large gold hoops that encircled the cheek with graceful pearl pendant dangling provocatively just above the inviting upper lip.

Tikka was a headpiece inserted through the hair partings and tied at the back. Its circular shape resting on the forehead of the bride giving it an extra face appeal.
This spot was believed to be the house of 'Ajana chakra', this center of energy or charka stood for preservation and steadfastness and thus by adorning herself a woman reiterated her status as the preserver of the human race. She became the source of continuity of human race and guardian of its moral values. So a virtuous woman became admired as a devi or a goddess

Payal or anklets with small jingling bells were tied around ankles and they omitted a pleasant musical sound as the lady walked. The other ornaments for the bride and for the groom's household consisted of earrings, pendants and rings. This sort of shopping took few days to accomplish as one had to be very careful when buying gold jewellery. One must be accompanied by an expert for testing the gold carats quality as there were bound to be some counter- feighting and cheating involved.

*

In The Days of Love

Throughout the history Indian sweetmeats had been a part and parcels of any celebrations or of auspicious days. Sophisticated varieties of these had been created to suit different pallets. Both sweets and salty saviouries had been order of the day and without this marriage celebration would be incomplete. So the initial planning is essential involving making of these sweets, for which an expert maker was to be involved, named halwai.

So a well known halwai was found and employed at the bride's place where he would set up his working space accompanied by his assistants. He would be in charge of all the menus for the marriage party, on three days of wedding feast.

Various sweets have their own cooking ingredients, which are carefully mixed and processed by an expert. Although most sweet dishes had radically different procedures of cooking but basically sugary syrup is used made in one set of pattern. Its consistency might however change from recipe to recipe. Consistency of sugar syrup is measured by the thread test. Whenever slightly cooled syrup was checked by pinch method between index finger and the thumb, if a thread was formed it meant that it had reached the required constancy. Gulab jamans, barfi, ladoos and jalebis are very popular among all the people. The sweets.Jalebis could be eaten hot or cold but it was tasted best when hot. The thick paste was made by mixing water and flour, with a pinch of saffron to give it an orange colour and then the thick paste was poured into tumbler which had a hole at its bottom. When the hot syrup in a metallic cauldron was ready, winding patterns of the paste were poured into the syrup and cooked. Thus those juicy syrupy sweets were formed.

Burfi was created from milk powder, grinded almonds and sugar. The hot paste was spread over an oily surfaced tray and when cooled, cut into rectangular slices.

Most of the sweets were served hot on the wedding feast but the spare quantities were saved to be distributed after the marriage to acquaintances in the bride's village. It was a custom to distribute these to all known people of the village and to all the workmen and other professional people. If a beggar or a holy man called at the door, it was customary to give them certain quantity.

Beside the sweets, there were quantities of savouries also to be served when the marriage party called at the tea reception where these were best served and enjoyed. These were normally of saltish taste called the namkeen and consisted of chewda, basin, pakoras, gathia and samosas. Hot pakoras and samosa were best eaten hot with tomato sauce or the sauces made out of tamarind water. The tamarind was soaked overnight and the resulting water was mixed with chillies to make it potent weapon for the tongue. Though having a burning mouth, people enjoyed its hot sourly sensation even if brought tears to their eyes. It was time to enjoy all the rich tastes of the foods at the feast.

*

When the news of her proposed marriage reached the ears of Sohni, it was a cruel blow that shattered her completely. She felt that her life had come to an end-a bitter end of enormous tragedy. Consequently she lost all the taste for life-her enthusiasm and motivation. She was a girl of great energy and was always on the go but now she came to realize hollowness of her hopes and all her enterprises. She sought the refuge of her room and locked herself in, in the total darkness of her being. Sight of a human face simply brought back all those emotions of emptiness. Hemmed in by inaction and as it happened she sought for the moments of sleep, the little brother of death, where nothing mattered but peaceful oblivion. Even this was not possible to achieve. She found even in her sleep there was no escape from dreadful reality as her thoughts took shapes of nightmares.

 And how one could escape from those? She could not envisage any solution. She realized that behind those nightmare there was her consciousness which gave her a feeling for sense of being and in order to erase her nightmares, she had to erase her consciousness and which was an awful enterprise. One could seize to exist but how? By ending one's life but then what? Her consciousness might survive. So there was no solution either in her life and or in death. But if she killed herself she would never be able to see Karan a. Against all the odds she was sure that by looking at his face she could touch that mysterious territory of life and which would save her from that abyss. These might be her mere fantasies but it was all she possessed in her hour of darkness. She could not afford to lose these- her last and the greatest possession. She must pick herself up and go to see Karan. She had not seen him for last three days and he would surely be worried about her.

 Actually he was sick with worrying constantly. He was going in vicious circles thinking of dark happenings. Had Sohni ceased to love him? If she turned herself away from him, what would he do then? A deep panic seized him and he felt sick to the core and he thought of going to her house to call upon her but turned back halfway due to lack of courage. He recently had seen her uncle hovering about in the village. If he called at the house and suppose her uncle was there, it would only exacerbate the situation and put her even under more pressure. He took the cattle on their grazing round and waited for her for days but she never showed up. He was sure that she had deserted him and all was lost.

Sohni used to bring him food to appease his hunger but now he had no hunger left and no inclination to cook for himself. He felt weaker and weaker and one day a farmer's wife taking pity on him, gave him something to eat and it somehow sustained him for the time being. His only consolation was his music and he played on his flute repeatedly and the sound of melancholy voices spread over the village and open spaces.

One day after recovering slightly from her predicaments, she prepared some food and came to see him. They were overwhelmed with emotions and at the sight of each other burst into tears and went into a warm embrace to seek solace from each other. When she told him the news about his proposed marriage though terrible it did not affect him too much as he suspected it somehow instinctively. In his heart he always suspected that such things were bound to happen but did not want to confront it and was hoping against hope that such dreadful things would never appear.

He was mad emotionally with Sohni's love and believed his life to be but a small stake in that game of love. He thought that love was greater than his own life. He was ready to bet his life in that game of love. He thought that one single moment, one single day full of her closeness was worth thousands lives like his without any love. So he clung to her tightly, his mind effused with the warmth of her body. His love and his soul were alive and that was more important to him at that moment than any other promise of future happiness. Listening to sweet words of his beloved, he tried to overcome the barriers of darkness and dejection. As long as they both were alive there was always a hope and the hope was to turn his thoughts into deeds, which would infuse more energy into the lethargic states of their lives.

Clinging to each other they sat there immobile till desire became incandescent . Sohni pulled him to her lap and held him clasped even tighter and he had obtained the most desired-a kiss, a kiss that would act like a catalyst to reanimate their bond with a promise of even closer intimacy. There was a state of mind in which they lost any sense of time and with it their remembrances of past especially Karan who had bitter memories of his past .Each sought the refuge of their mouths to appease their anguish and as it fired with the moisture of the kiss and that kiss yielded to them the hidden recesses of their souls. But it was getting dark and they had to leave each other soon. They wanted to prolong their stay together a little more. Sohni was afraid that someone might notice her absence and might come searching for her and once they found her in close proximity of her lover the hell was going to lose. They had to entangle their embrace.

From emotional high they drifted towards their rationality and tried to be brave through empowerment of their souls. What was going to happen to their lives? One terrible choice suggested to their minds- an option to take leave off their lives in company of each other. Perhaps take some sort of poison or jump together in some deep waters or in the river just flowing past the village. After pondering on such cruel fate, they decided against it for the time being. It was cowardly to leave the world just like that as they had not even explored all the possibilities- an escape from the bondages imposed on them by others. It was hard for Sohni to give herself away body and soul to other man. Under the love of her father and demands for social convention, she might be forced to yield her body but not her soul, and no way was she going to do that in any circumstances.

Even if she was married, they would find a way to see each other somehow and keep their contacts and their souls alive with the spark of hope alive in their hearts.

*

After so many complicated preparations and arrangements, the marriage day was nearly there. The ladies from the bride's side set the auspicious mood rolling about a month's before the marriage. All the singers and dancers congregate at her house in the evenings to introduce a mood of gaiety with singing and dancing. As usual they performed the music accompanied by harmonium and dholak or a drum for rhythmical accompaniment to the singing. The ladies of the village took initiative in organizing the group. They introduce songs from old traditions as well as from the modern resources. The lead singer led the way and then the other joined in to perform community singing. It was an occasion for initiating the gaiety for the approaching wedding day, setting a mood for hearts resounding music and high energy. As the singing party got warm the dancers stepped in. Kikkli was a special dance performed by two girls holding hands and twirling each other in circles and balancing their positions with circular motions. Other ladies encouraged them to go faster and faster, by clapping and singing to add vigorous rhythms.

*

A special ceremony of jaggo took place in the late hours of the night before the wedding day, an event into which close relatives and friends were invited. It was the task of the maternal relatives of the bride to assemble and to make the arrangements for the ceremony. They decorated a copper vessel called gaffer with divas (lamps) made of atta (wheat flour). They lighted these lamps with mustard oil and wicks. The bride's maternal aunt carried the vessel on her head and started walking around the village. Another lady carried a long stick with ghungroos or small jingling bells tied at top and lead the procession by striking the stick on the ground thus producing pleasing musical sounds indicating the arrival of the procession. They called on every house and were greeted at each, with offerings of sweetmeats. The householders poured more oil to keep the lamps burning. A vigorous dance of gidda was performed accompanied by enthusiastic clapping from the gathered crowd.

The display of burning of small lamps and the ladies dressed in colourful clothes and their dances added a glamorous spectacle to the darkness of the night. Encouraged by this play, the children goaded by adults brought their fireworks and set it off to add spectacular display of high sounds and fiery bursts. All this gaiety and colorful expressions delighted everyone and would have gone all night but for the reason that they had to keep their alertness to the full for the following morning when the actual wedding ceremony was going to start.

*

On the groom's side, invitations were issued to relations and friends as to join in the wedding party and one was careful as not to miss any prominent person, otherwise one had to face grievances and complaints for rest of the life. When the final count was scrutinized, the number came to nearly to hundred and which was a large party. which Vehicles were to be hired for traveling to the bride's place.

Arrangements were made to have the marriage party staying there for full two nights. Rooms were hired in hotels and inns to accommodate the guests, making sure that their rooms were up to the standard and their beds to be clean and tidy. A special person was assigned to the party for looking after the guests and their needs. The party hired their own musicians and a band troupe, mainly of brass instruments. The party had to travel each day from their accommodations to the bride's reception for dinner and evening meals. Their breakfast and evening teas were arranged at their own accommodations.

Freshly prepared sweetmeats, saviouries, milk and tea etc were carried for the guests and they had plenty of choice in choosing the eatables they liked. Hot Jalebis, ladoos and gulab jamans were the favourites of the day and people who liked the namkeens or salty dishes went for samosas, pakoras and other such things. These were made of gram flours with fillings and fried in hot oil. The smell of all these goodies was overpowering for the guests and all those hungry souls fell upon the dishes like they would never again have the chance to eat these for the rest of their lives.

Everyone was pleased with their reception and with their first taste of special foods prepared for them. There were more promises of greater things to come at dinner at night and on the following days. After indulging themselves heavily they were reminded that their dinners were still outstanding and they should go easy and leave some room in their bellies for that. All they wanted then was to take some rest for a nap to digest their food and then prepare for their evening procession to the house of the bride for dinner.

In the evening when the darkness descended, the marriage party procession started, fronted by musician and a brass band that were playing the popular tunes of the day. People were in their finest clothes, gaudy and colourful. Their multicolored array of turbans was a sight to behold and attracted a large crowd of seers from the village. As it was their first venture, they decided to cover all the streets of the village via their procession. Stopping at each square the band gave a rigorous display of their talents and virtuosity of the instruments they played upon. The gathered crowd was much entertained and they showed their appreciation by long cheers.

When the groom's barat reached the reception venue, a milni or uniting ceremony was performed. The bride's close relatives gave a warm welcome to the groom and his relatives with flower garlands and rose water being sprinkled on them to usher in an atmosphere of freshness and perfumed elegance and then the milni ceremony was performed. It was performed in the descending order of the personal ages, beginning with the elder most. In absence of any living grand dads, it were the perspective fathers from both sides.

The fathers hugged each other and gave gifts of clothes and money to each other. The second turn being of respective brothers from both sides and so on. The idea being a sort of introduction and getting to know each other on a personal level. A ceremony for present and future uniting of two families. Laughter and jokes were exchanged to break the solemnity and it made the atmosphere conducive to feasts and celebrations. Everyone from the wedding party was shown to their seats for the dinner to commence.

It was made sure that everything went smoothly and there were no hitches, unpleasantries or frictions. Usually it was normal for the guests to get drunk and behave badly -there were free drinks available to all the people present. When people got drunk, it was loutish behaviour to show themselves off by shouting or by finding faults with the food served. People with experience to deal with such mishaps were recruited before hand and usually these were the elders from the villages and people from bride's side and groom's side mutually assisted each other.

The first evening meal was to be served to the crowd for which numerous volunteers were recruited beforehand and these being relations and friends of the bride's family. These people were volunteers and were giving their services free just for the love of it. There was bewildering varieties of food available and the difficult task was to contact each individual as to his/her choice. Some were vegetarians while others being non-vegetarians adding complicity to food distribution.

The first course was for fruit juices, teas, lassis, sweetmeats etc. These were taken in moderation as for the main course to arrive, for the vegetarians there were aloo gobi, brinjal bhaji, matter paneer, cauliflowers, potatoes, sarson saag, etc together with cooked pulses such as mung, mash, lentils to be consumed with roti, paratha, naan or rice pillows. For added taste a verity of pickles, papadoms and sauces were made available.

Non vegetarians had their fill with rogan josh, chicken masala, bryani rice and chicken tandoori. Drinks of iced water, sherbets, mango lassi or fruit juices were served. Fresh rotis and naans were much in demand and a man with a basketful of these went around to satisfy additional demands. Sweet dishes, kulfi, ice creams etc were served at the end of the meals. Some people asked for hot cups of tea and coffee. It was a highly enjoyable feast and all the barattis were full of praise and congratulated the host for providing such an array of tasty foods and stated they were looking forward to other meals to come on the following day. Their only concern being that at the end of marriage they were going to put on   extra amount of weight and they had to shed it through hard work and physical exercises afterwads as otherwise it would be looked upon as the 'fatties' by their respective partners and for some unmarried, it could be a bar in netting a beautiful bride.

So the marriage celebrations went on the following day. Nowhere was the unique diversity of the country more evident that in marriage ceremonies and traditions. With multitudes of fashions, fabrics, customs and bridal make up playing a prominent role in making the bride feel on top of the world on that occasion and for the unification with her groom in front of sacred book and taking of the marriage wows. An important wedding tradition that had stood the test of time was the use of henna for adornments on hands and feet of the bride. Connected with ladies, the art of applying henna known as mehdi went back as far as thousands of years and most young women were still keen to apply it to their bodies. Even though mehdi is a green powder but when mixed with water and applied to skin, it took on a reddish orange hue.

Ladies specializing in make up for the bride came forward to beautify Sohni on the night before the ceremony. They applied the wet paste in intricate designs on her hands and feet and on the following morning friend and relations came to prepare the bride for the marriage ceremony. Gram flour mixed with milk was applied to her face and which when dry was peeled off giving her face a fresh and shinning look. After the application of the foundation lotions, other cosmetic preparations were applied to enhance the contours of her face and giving it a blushing look. Eye makeup had a special place in giving a stunning outlook as a woman's eyes could cast a seductive spell on her husband and win his heart through enchantment of her beauty and physical appeal.

On the third day after the breakfast the religious ceremony took place and it was called Anand Karaj, as a union of two souls which was a prescribed form for their religion and literary meant as 'Blissful Union'. This religious ceremony was special as two individual were going to be joined in equal partnership. It was joyus and festive event, which was very family orientated and informal in its atmosphere. The Rehat Maryada code under which the marriage was conducted stated that any sort of dowry arrangements were forbidden but common people did not understand it and did not applied it strictly to themselves and most marriages involved fell into a business transactions.

The ceremony was going to be performed at home and so the house was turned into a sort of temple with the holy book installed on a pedestal and behind which the officiating priest sat. It started early in the morning with the ragis or the group of musicians performed shabads or sacred hymns to usher in an atmosphere of piety and good omen. The three ragis sat on a dais and sang hymns from the holy book in tune to the harmoniums on which they operated, accompanied by a table player to add the percussions. The holy book was decked in profusion of romalas or garments and a passageway was made for people to come to give their respects to the holy book. They bowed to the holy book or touched their foreheads to the ground in front and put some currency or coins in money box as offerings.

At the appointed time the groom came and sat in front looking splendid in his pink turban and matching sherwani waiting for the bride to arrive. At nod of the priest the bride was ushered in supported by her father and brother. She came and sat next to the groom. The priest recited ardas or the prayer followed by kirtan(musical hymns sung for marriage ceremony). The groom followed by his bride had to go around the holy book a number of times to the chantings of the priest and who tied a piece of cloth over the groom's shoulder to the garments of the bride as signifying the tying of knot.

The priest recited:

"On the first round

A union of two souls

The servant of God proclaims that this is the first round of the marriage ceremony and
The ceremony has begun."

The groom and bride go around the holy book, the bride guided by her brothers and relations.

"On the second round of the ceremony, The Lord leads you to true Guru, The primal Being.

With the fear of God, be fearless in mind.

Eradicate the littleness of your ego.

In The Days of Love

The Lord, the supreme soul who is pervading everywhere.

Fully filling all the spaces

Remember the Lord."

"Deep within, and without, there is only one Lord.

Meeting together, the servants of the lord sing thy songs of joy.

As I speak the words of Lord's in the Bani."

*

After the marriage ceremony there was general all round relief that everything went well except for Sohni who had to go through the whole ceremony without feeling any joy or happiness. She was just carrying out his father's wishes as did not want to hurt him on account of so called family's honour; by refusing to marry her chosen suitor. She was crying most of the time and people took it to be traditional mood of the bride as they were going through the motion of breaking all old to her old family and establishing new connection to the in laws of the new family.

There was gaiety too in the old customs of playing practical jokes on the groom and to which ordeal he had to go through keeping and who were anxious to perform as many puns on him as practically possible, without really annoying him. He was invited to eat some sweets which were an imitation and made to look like the real ones. They were usually made of clay but painted with all the fruit's colours and when groom tried to bite into these , he bit into clay with a mouthful of foul taste. He might be invited to sit on a chair with only three legs and when he fell there were general merriment among the girls. Sometime his shoes got stolen and he had to pay a heavy monetary price to get them back. It was a part of general celebrations and no one got angry or upset.

 The dowry goods were put on display for the general public- all the jewelry, garments, gifts, furniture which was given by parents to be taken by the bride to her new home. Old women came and scrutinize everything with cunning eyes, passing remarks on each item.

The final phase of the ceremony came when the bride was ready to depart. It was the most poignant part and all her friends and relations were on the verge of tears with heavy hearts. The parents who had brought up their little girl with care, love and even hardships were on the verge of breaking all their old ties and she had to leave for an alien land with different life away from them. To them it was simply heart rending.

As the poet said:

"Now the time has come for my heart break

 A last look to for my old companions

The trees of my childhood

 Who were always present

To give me solace each time

Happy that I climbed to their tops

And felt like a princess of high

In The Days of Love

Nevermore I will touch them again.

All the open fields and the river

Birds of the air will miss me

And shed tears on my departure

Nevermore they will see me again.

My dear father who did not allow even a scratch

On my delicate skin

Look how he had abandoned me to my cruel fate
With wounds inflicted on all my heart

Dear father do not give me away

Keep me one more day

Closer to your heart again…"

Sohni went around to say farewell to all her dear friends and relations and clung to each sobbing. She had to be separated from each one. Her makeup became messy with heavy with tears, ruining all the make ups of her face, mascara and the delicate shadows inserted under her eyes.

Chapter Eight

The mother in law was waiting in her house in great anticipation, for the arrival of the new bride and all the village women had gathered also to greet the bride. They started a musical interlude, songs for the auspicious day, songs from old traditions, songs of new times giving expressions to high emotions of the human heart. Mother in law distributed sweets among them and her heart sang too, dancing in tune to the song women were singing.

At the sight of the bridal procession there was great commotion and noises, loud shouts and plenty of greetings. Mother in law stood in the doorway of the entrance to her house carrying a tumbler of oil, for prelude and a ritual for blessing her son and daughter in law. Women spilled out in the passageway and into the street to see the whole spectacle. Slowly the drove in and halted in front of the house and the groom stepped out and helped the bride to get out of out of the carriage. She was wrapped in a golden brocade dress with both her head and face covered. Mother in law hugged the bride and then her son while her heart thumped and fluttered with joy, embracing she took the bride to the doorway. Groom and bride stood together in front of her and she circled the oil filled vessel over the heads of bride and groom, praying for blessing, to be bestowed on the couple for their health, long life and for the union to be blessed with plenty of off-springs.

She guided the bride to the house and sat her on a chair where the crowd gathered. 'Mukh Dekhni' or the' face glimpsing' ceremony was performed. She put a fifty rupees note in bride's lap and lifted her veil, it was a pretty face and a dazzling one too and it made her heart brimming with joy. Other women followed repeating the procedure and all were struck with the bride's extraordinary beauty. Then the attention was turned to groom and he was heartily congratulated for acquiring a new wife and moreover getting such a pretty one. May the sun of fortune shine on the couple.

Hearing about that good news other women of the village poured in and soon a long line was formed for the ' face glimpsing ' which though was exciting for the onlookers but no so pleasant for the bride who had to face the staring gazes of those throng of women repeatedly. It was harder for her to bear if you are depressed and gloomy inward.

In the mean while all her dowry was unloaded and displayed in the courtyard, either spread out on the tables or on the makeshift beds and on other pieces of furniture. It was a rich and expensive display and everybody admired the generosity and expenses incurred by the bride's father. It was a normal custom to find faults with the given dowry but it did not happen there and which was unusual. Even the parents of the groom thought that it had exceeded their expectations. If the bride did not bring the expected loot, she had to bear that mark of infamy for the rest of her married life, being reminded again and again about the meanness of her parents.

After all these ceremonies, she had to suffer further ordeals and had to prove herself to be worthy bride for the groom especially on first night of the marriage. Women of the family were more prone to pay considerable attention to romantic and a sexual aspect as far as the first nights of the newlywed couples was concerned. The entrance to the marriage suit was hung with coloured papers of all sorts and the marital suite was decked very tastefully and the arrangements took considerable time to do. They paid a lavish attention to the bed where the first union was going to take place in due time. After the evening meal the bride was taken to the chamber and was told to undress and lie under a coverlet and wait for her husband.

The bride did not look forward to wedding night with any enthusiasm but the groom was filled with anxiety, nervousness and hesitation and many questions kept creeping at the back of his mind. He entered the chamber and felt a sweet smell wafting around in the room as the woman had sprayed some fine perfumes all around. Garlands of marigold were hanging above the bridal bed and the bed itself was strewn with petals of roses. He took off his clothes and felt embarrassed to be completely naked and so he left the under wears on. He slipped himself slowly onto the bed, lifted the coverlet and put his body next to her. His heart was thumping and he tried to listen to the breathing of the person lying next to him. He extended his arm and touched her body but was surprised to find her fully clothed. He was not pleased.

He touched her lips with fingers but there was no anxious quiver there but pair of cold wet flesh. Slowly his fingers explored her cheeks and touched her eyes. The bride was crying with silent sobs. He tried to embrace her but she moved away. He felt awkward, uncomfortable and in order to overcome his humiliation he began to fantasize…. He was kissing her gently and she responded and opened her mouth to taste his mouth, they were exploring each other's body and each one explored their naked flesh and held their members to squeeze and…. she was opening herself to high erotic sensations…. That act involved the mind, body and soul of the couple and created irresistible magnetism between the two… but.

It was a disaster and nothing sexual happened between them and the groom swallowed   the bitter pill. He began to weep for himself, weeping thus he exhausted himself and somehow went to sleep. In order to solace himself he began to muse:

'It always happens on first night.'

'Do not worry, she will come around it.'

In The Days of Love

'It is her first experience and she is bound to be shy.'

He was a macho man and must not be discouraged by his first attempt. He was capable of great sexual performances .He was bitter inside but kept smiling.

Surinder, the husband, had looked forward to marriage and which led to an imaginary land where the musical name of Sohni was ringing and reverberating in mindscapes of his thoughts. He wanted to take her into his arms and travel through winding roads of his estate and halt at intervals to listen to the tinkling of her anklet bells and all the muffled noises of the vast space. To greet the sunshine of the morning in her embrace and taste the golden respite of the sunsets at evening. To stand under the clear skies of the night and give thanks for the starry heavens and to pay tribute to blissful paradise of his love.

And all that seemed a dream and forever it would remain out of his reach.

Sohni had no such dream about her married life. Her dreams only reached the realms of love for Karan and ended there. Beside these she had no enthusiasm left for anything else but she still she had to exist, whatever the circumstances may be. The secret desire in her heart had never died and possibility of a contact with Karan always existed and for that privilege she had to survive somehow. To overcome the depression and lethargy of her mind, she began to take more interest in the running of her household as there were so many chores waiting to be performed. She became friendly with a young female servant employed in the household and began to confide in her the secrets of her past.

She began to apply her previous experiences gained at father's house in managing the estate and took inventory of all the stocks at her new home and at the farm. She opened an account book and began to record all the transactions which included all the outgoings -wages paid to the employees, purchase of new farm equipment and animals. She assessed and projected the income for the coming year. Her father- in-law and mother-in-law were delighted and marveled at the talents of their new bride. She began to show positive side of nature to the villagers and obtained their respect and confidence. It was all very well but she could not bring herself to surrender anyway to Surrinder sexually. People could see that he had changed and the person whom they found to be extrovert and of happy disposition began to turn broody and of gloomy. He did not divulge his grievances to anybody even to his parents, as he was ashamed to show that he was having problems in the bed. People might get wrong ideas as instead of blaming Sohni, they might think of him as a man not good enough to satisfy his wife. Outwardly they put a show that they were sleeping together but inwardly they began to drift apart. They hated each other's guts. Each night was an ordeal to go through and they slept back to each other and their gap in sleeping positions began get wider and wider.

Anybody who was sensitive could perceive their marital problems and would have concluded that the marriage was ushering in hellish times and pitied them for leading such a miserable married life.

*

Sohni's marriage was a terrible blow to Karan. During the marriage ceremony he simply lost his nerve and lay in his quarters day and night pondering on his cruel fate. Whenever he heard the distant sounds of the bands leading the baraat, he simply covered his ears with his hands and blocked all the musical sounds coming out. He gave a notice to his employer about termination of his employment and left the village in order to break any connection with it and get away from it all., with all the associations of the past.

He wanted to die but the hope of meeting with his beloved again, could not let him die. His sufferings taught him to distance himself from all the worldly things and to which other people clung to and catered for all their lives .He wanted to become a sadhu , in order to face the despair of living and forget about all the false comforts and promises for life given by the worldly philosophers. He saw that around him all was suffering. Though in his childhood he had caught glimpses of happiness in company of his father but when he died his world collapsed. One was always dependent on a single person for his happiness and which seemed so false. When one is surrounded by pleasant things, one never considered the meaning of existence and then that solidity and assurance was suddenly removed from under your feet and you fell flat on your face. Such was the nature of things.

Sadhus were often called sanyasi or renunciates, who had left behind all material and sexual attachments of the world but which makes the bedrock foundation of the worldliest people of the world. Sadhus tried to live away from human habitations like in caves, forests or wilderness or even in temples and which were tolerant towards them. Some lived in ashrams amid urban population and supplemented their paltry income by giving psycho-spiritual cures, officiating at marriages, births or funerals and sometime helping with children's education.

A sadhu was usually addressed as' baba' by the common folks. The word 'baba' means 'father 'or a respectable elder. Sometime the respectful suffix 'Ji ' was also added as 'babaji' to give it a mark of respect. There were millions of them spread across the breadth and length of the country. They were usually respected and revered but also feared for any curses they might put on people whom they did not like. They were considered the bearer of the collective karma of the society and by austerities they might burn the bad and sinful karma of the people. This beneficial aspect was respected and supported by donations from many people.

The weakness of the concept of saduship being that so many beggars and cheats   also donned themselves as such, in order to beg and make money in towns or places of pilgrimage and thus giving bad name to the real ones.

They engaged in a wide variety of religious practices. Some practiced extreme form of
Asceticism while others focused on prayers, chanting and meditations. They were divided into various sects and which could be numerious and of bewildering variety. Shaiva sadhus were devoted to god Shiva while the Vaishnava sadhus belonged to god Vishnu. There were also the Shakta sadhus who worshipped goddess Shakti or the female divine energy.

In classical Sanskrit literature human life's span of hundred years was divided into four segments the last phase of twenty five years was assigned to renunciation of the world and worldly things and in pursuits of detachment, this was not always the case as anyone could take sadhuship at any age. Most people come to it through their experiences of bad family connections, financial troubles or heart breakage due to unhappy love affairs. The processes and rituals of becoming a sadhu were different for each sect but in almost all the sects a sadhu was initiated by a guru who bestowed upon the initiate a new name as well as a mantra or a sacred sound. This mantra which was a private phrase only known to the sadhu and to be repeated by the initiate as part of meditative practices. The guru was an important figure in all these ascetic traditions and was often equated with a deity .The service rendered to one's guru, however menial in form, was considered as an important part of the spiritual practices.

In The Days of Love

The real life of an ascetic was rugged and hard, denying pleasures and comforts of normal life and which deterred many from either taking it on or leaving the order after a brief period. Practices of a sadhu consisted of obligatory early morning rising, taking cold bath even in high mountains amid frozen snows and complete detachments from common practices of ordinary life After the bath sadhus congregated in a group to perform rituals for the prayers and long meditative practices. Solitary sadhu meditated in caves, wilderness or even in the cremation grounds-their aim being detachment and to see the fragility of human life as always confronting death.

The aim of an earnest sadhu being a detachment from the physical body and surroundings which gave him some sort of immunity from desires and attachments to flesh. They slept on hard surfaces and some eccentric even on a bed of nails, stood on one leg for considerable time or even for years or some crawled on the ground over long distances. Some took things to extreme, denouncing even their clothes and becoming naked ascetics or nanga sadhus. They covered their bodies with ashes as a mark of complete detachments from body.

There were regular melas or festivals of getting together, meetings when thousands congregated along banks of the holy rivers and where they exchanged views and experiences and helped the pilgrims with religious intricacies leading to moksha or liberation from the sansara. Often they lived on donations from lay people but there life was often hard and precarious where poverty and hunger were always present and their future being always uncertain, the monsters of starvation and death ever present. The life of a sadhu called for celibacy, self imposed long silence, poverty and solitude.

The genuine sadhus radically renounced 'this world' in order to focus entirely on the higher realities beyond. They abstained from sex, cut all family ties, had no possessions, no house, wore little or no clothing and ate little but simple food. For an ordinary human being these 'basic' self-abnegations were hard to comprehend. But almost unimaginable were the extreme austerities — even self-mortifications — by which a number of sadhus intended to speed up their enlightenment.

The time of bhakti yoga or devotional yoga brought about some female devotees
too and which might be called sadhvis or sadhnis who worshipped Krishna of their inner being. Meera was one of these and though married in a royal family, her heart was in giving devotion and her life to Krishna and composed songs in his praises. She danced and sang in temples expounding her humanistic philosophy of peace and loving, much to the annoyance of the royal. Absorbed in her devotional mind she forgot about everything, herself and all the world and its rules and rituals.

She was traveling all over the country preaching the name of the lord and came to a river and wanted to cross it to the other shore but had no money. She urged the boatman to take her across 'in the name of lord' and the boatman laughed at that foolish woman.

'I take people only in the name of mammon, if you are so inclined why don't you cross by yourself in the name of lord.'

And it was said that in her innocent way, she just walked across the water to the other shore. Boatman and spectator were thunder struck with amazement and dread.

*

After Sohni's marriage Karan lost his whole world. Once he had touched a dimension saturated with bubbling ocean of life, a richness that was beyond his comprehension and

142

having experiences that he had never known in his life. He was amazed at those passions, capable of creating a new reality of existence and it resounded with a vastness of his inner being and further it not only comprised his inner world but the outer world too and it was that miracle which was so incomprehensible to him. But now he felt that he had been exiled from that unknown country.

He realized that a further logical analysis would not take him towards any understanding of loving a woman like Sohni but the so called an irrational approach would be more useful and would decipher a meaningful comprehension of his enigma. 'Love' might be knowable and comprehensible feeling to some people buy but did not mean that a sentence such as 'I love you.' could be wholly analyzed in known terms of logical language. One had to create a new language derived from one's experience and there was the rub. No one would explain his love for her even when he did his best to explain it.

Contrary to accepted rules the lovers did not give up their individual identities in the so called union of lovers but on the contrary could enhance the autonomy of each and promote growth of new talents for love and loving. It gave dignity to each other and brought out meaningful sensation to each and somehow made them teach to be a true person.

He thought about where to go next and it was the second time he was being uprooted from a place which he thought to be a 'home' for himself and where he had some meaningful existence but now he was being banished from it again. He had to repeat the same journey which he did sometime ago when leaving his ancestral home. He started again walking by the river or through the countryside and had no idea what he was looking. He met man in saffron cloth and started talking to that person and asked for some advice.

The man told him of a nearby dera which few sadhus had made as their abode and that he should visit it and may be stay there temporarily. He went there and saw the head sadhu or the guru and poured his heart to him and the guru was sympathetic to his plight and told him about the conditions of a sadhu's life. He invited him to stay at his place and ponder about the future course of his life. He stayed there for few days and a plan began to take shape in his mind. He had not much left in his life except the love of Sohni and which had become his emotional weakness and limitation. He could not do anything about it and he had to accept it. For a drowning man this was the last straw thrown to him and he had to accept it.

A certain auspicious day was chosen by his guru for his initiation into sadhuhood and on that day he got up early in the morning and had a bath. A religious ceremony was performed and under a canopy of mantras, he was initiated into sadhuhood and a new identity was bestowed upon him with a new name. As normal initiates he did not had any ties to break and it was easy for him to enter his punar janam or 'new birth'. Saffron robes were going to be his garb in the future and with a turban to match. He was also given a secret mantra of his own, which to recite when he was meditating. The guru expounded the techniques and rituals of meditation that he had to carry out for long hours in the morning and other suitable times of the day.

He found it easy to do long sessions in meditation and it was a welcome diversion from the gloomy state of his mind. He realized soon that it was god sent boon to relieve his mind of all the dark dross he was carrying in his mind as otherwise his mind might have cracked sending to some lunatic asylums. Voluntarily he would engage his mind on certain aspects of meditations and visualizing peaceful deities and tried to identify with those while breathing calmly and deeply .Whenever he got stuck or dejected, he had to seek the help of his guru and which was not so easy as the guru was mostly out or instructing other sadhus or to some lay people from the villages nearby. The guru also helped people with simple physical sicknesses or implied some esoteric methods for relieving serious mental or physical diseases. He realized that he was on the first rung of the ladder and had much to learn. In the meantime the guru instructed him to do other physical chores to keep his mind and body in order, He began to look after the whole premises of the dera. It had a big compound and number of rooms which needed sweeping and washing constantly.

Some time their food was prepared in the common kitchen provided they had sufficient provisions and enough flour to make chapattis as otherwise they had to go to the adjoining villages and call on the householders for food and alms. The sadhus did not own anything material except their begging bowl and depended upon other people for food or some small denotations.

*

Both Karan and Sohni were in the same state of mind as if in a sort of communion with each other. The emotional energies from their minds were pouring out into the space and each one was the receptor of each other .Separation and longing for each other were creating a sort a fog in their hearts and t both had to cope with it without being overwhelmed by it and thus going under. New actions were needed to combat those oceans of misery.

 Neither Sohni nor her husband were satisfied with their conjugal lives as she could not give herself fully to her husband and his desires as she felt a sort of betrayal to the memory of Karan and their past loving episodes which were strongly entrenched in her mind. She felt strongly attached to him and her first love was more like a spiritual marriage and a full surrender to her husband was a sort of unfaithfulness to her. Both suffered inwardly and began to sleep in separate beds but kept it a secret from the family. Only her faithful maid knew something of that rift and which Sohni confided in her as the secrets were safe with her.

She had a knack of making new friends and as previously in her unmarried state. She began to form a close group of females of her age who met regularly in each other's house and talked about mutual interests and hobbies, housewife's work and grudges against the in-laws. They also indulged in their hobbies of dress- making, basketry and music making. They found a way of lessening their drudgery of day to day routine work and enlivened it with creative activities. Mother-in laws were pleased as there was less traditional bickering among daughter in laws and mother in laws, due to their engagements. In the traditional farming families it was expected that the bride would soon get pregnant and bear plenty of off-springs as to assist with the farm work when the children grew up. So marriage was considered as a sort of insurance against the shortage of farm labour to help in tilling the land. Here the male gender had preference over the female infants. The girls did not really belong to their maternal families and as soon as they were grown up into womanhood, they were ready for their weddings. And move away.

The birth of a female child was not welcomed in most families and when such event occurred, it was a sad occasion as such birth only brought burden on the father. He had to educate the girl and then start saving for her dowry and as a result he is financially and emotionally enslaved, this he could inwardly feel despite his upfront of well being. There were few mutterings sometime against such malpractices but generally people adhered to long established traditions, which had become the foundations of their social structures. This could lead to inferior status of women in the traditional societies and especially in the home lives and treatment of married women.

*

Karan began to take up more and more of his sadhuship's duties. The guru took him everywhere as his assistant and he liked his non assertive nature and the capacity to learn quickly. There were so many poor families who could not afford any paid medical treatments and so depended on sadhu's dera for such emergencies. The guru after years of such practice had acquired certain knowledge of herbs and potions and carried such with him in his medicinal bag. He showed Karan as how to approach a sick person, examine and diagnose him/her. It was an expert job, which was to be learnt gradually over number of years.

The patients were administered with medicinal doses, usually in powder form, wrapped in small bundles of paper made from some old newspapers. If the householder could afford a small price for the medicines, it was well and good ,otherwise the medicines were given free. It was a usual custom to provide food or cooked meals to the visitors including the sadhu and his medical assistant. Dera people realized soon that part of the cure consisted in giving assurances that the medicine would work and this had a great beneficial effect on the patient's recovery.

The ultimate aim of sadhuship being moksha or liberation from the suffering of this life. This purification of the mind was brought about through meditation, service of sick and needy but the true purification meant the purification of five physical elements associated with body-earth, water, fire, air and space. Fire was the most preferred element and it was kept burning perpetually in sadhu's dera as it was considered the destroyer of all the ills, associated with human body and mind.

The sadhus survived on meager diets of cereal products and fruit and were not bothered where the next meal was coming from. They went around the villages and human habitations to beg for their food and took everything that was given to them voluntarily. They were instructed as not to beg beyond their physical needs and usually turned to their abode when this condition was fulfilled as regarding their physical needs. Whenever food was given, they blessed the householder and prayed for their prosperity and well being.

These were not always the norms especially if the sadhu or the householder happened to be sensitive and prone to take offense against any rude language used. Some householders became so fed up with constant bickering of the beggars at their doors that they verbally abused them or set their dogs on them It went the other way around too and the sadhus of bad temperaments threatened to put a curse on the householder who declined to give them any alms or when they were given stale or infested food.

*

Karan tried to lose himself in his work in his new role of a sadhu. He meditated earnestly and tried to detach himself from all his past but found it hard going. He made a point of visiting sick and needy in the afternoons, engaging them in mutual active talks as to assist them in finding a solution to their predicaments. He was learning the science of herbal medicines from his guru and which he employed in his treatment for the sick people he was visiting and if the case was serious, he sought help from his guru. But in spite of all these engagements he was still living in the past with all its emotional reaction. He found out that his love for Sohni had gone too deep inside him and had taken roots in his heart and had spread far and wide. Soon the dictates of his heart overpowered his intellectual resolves. After sometime he resolved to go to the village where Sohni was now living. He would stay at the dera for another month and help the guru to run the place as he owed him something for all the kindness and care he had shown him during his dark days. He began to grow his beard and to change his appearances as not to detected or recognized.

After a month he left the dera and made his way to the village by walking, which took him two days to reach. On the outskirt of the village he found a farmer's abandoned hut and made it as his temporary habitation. He did not want to make things hard for Sohni and so he meditated for three days to calm his mind. He donned his saffron robes and turban and with his growth of beard, he was sure that he would be unrecognizable. One sunny morning he went around the village asking for alms. It was big village and he had to find the exact house of his beloved. It took him time to find her house and then he kept a watch to make sure that her husband was out whenever he called.

One day when he saw the husband going out, he started calling at village houses for alms and eventually called on the desired house and a maid answered the sadhu's call.

' Alakh! Niranjan.' He gave out the religious call.

'What do you want?' The maid asked him, although she knew that the sadhu was asking for alms.

'Give some food to a hungry sadhu.'

'What do you want –some flour to make the chapattis with?'

'It will be better if you could give me some cooked meal.'
'I am still cooking, come back in an hour.'

As Karan was anxious to have a glimpse of Sohni, he returned to the house at the appointed time and was given some nice meal to eat. He thanked the maid and asked him if he could do anything in return and she told him that she was worried about the health of her mistress, she was depressed and not eating well. The sadhu suggested that he would call back in two days time and if the mistress cared to be seen, he might have a cure for her.

The maid reported the whole incident and her conversation with the sadhu to Sohni as she was curious to know all the details about the stranger. Sohni further asked the maid about her impressions of him and she replied that he seemed to be somewhat sincere and trustworthy though appearances could be deceptive. To further probing the maid replied that the sadhu was of fairly young age and she personally found him attractive. They both thought that it would be a good idea at least to see him when he called next, as no harm was involved and then assess the situation.

At the end of two days, the sadhu called at lunch time as promised earlier and the maid was expecting him and on asking him for alms or a meal, he was given a course of meals and for which he thanked the maid.

'Do not thank me. I am here only as a maid. My mistress provided you with a meal.'

' I thank her too and would like to thank her in person if she is willing to come to the door.' Sadhu requested slyly.

'Wait a minute and I will see if she can come out to see you.'

Sohni was hesitant to come out but eventually after delay she came out.

In The Days of Love

This was the first time Karan had seen her after her marriage, a wave of love and agony ran through his body. He wanted to hold her and hug her passionately but that was not possible. He had to conceal his identity in front of the maid. Sohni looked at him and a feeling of some past remembrances came to her, which she dismissed as another fantasy of her mind. Her face was withdrawn and sad.

'Mistress I thank thee for the meal I just received from your household.'

'There is no need to thank me. A sadhu needs to eat.'

'Mistress you look sad and unhappy. May I ask you the reason for it?'

'What is the use of wasting my breath. I am incurable.'

She wanted to say so many things, scream out her agony, only if it was possible.

But all her feelings became locked in her being.

She wanted to express:

I was the moonlit night of lapid love
Some confused lores of a tortured mind
A tongue to tell, to speak of truth jogia
Then to live in shades of encumbered lies.

No soul enamoured in this wide world
That can bring about my heart's satiation

Certainty within my soul will never again
Gaze upon starred face of Karan yaar

And never again the buds of my heart
Blossom anew in cloudy tales of romance.

Strike uproariously for hindered desire
Some deeds in burning to quench the fire.

I will sell my skull for vessel to be made
My dark tresses for silken rope to be woven
My gory skin for the shoes to be soled
And gauged eyes to blinds for instructions.

Oh my lord if my heart was not so worn
Glimpse of Karan yaar was enough
To restore my soul.

Forgive me dear God for sins of love
For seeds of grief, for songs for the dove
I will scatter my ashes windward to spark
On some altered dedicated to my true Lord.

Sensing her loss and all her inner tumults, Karan addressed her

'Mistress! Do not be so despondent and do not lose heart. Things are going to change and change for better.'

'Do not give me false hopes and do not lie to my face.'

' A sadhu does not lie. But mistress you are going to find your missing love.' Karan regretted but spelled it out.

Sohni looked at him in surprise and shock.

'If you meet me at my dera in the fields yonder, in company of your maid, I will be able to disclose a secret.'

In The Days of Love

Sohni looked at him with certain disbelief.

'Trust me mistress. You will find what you are looking for.'

The sadhu moved away leaving Sohni in suspense and shock.

*

After few days the maid called and told sadhu that his mistress would be coming soon to see him and after receiving this news, his heart was fluttering with a mixture of excitement, a possible disaster or renewal of love ties. When Sohni and her maid arrived they were taken inside that depilated building where make shift seats were made for them to sit.
The party brought some food and provisions for sadhu. They were eager to listen to the news from him as promised earlier.

'I gather you have lost a loved one and are eager to meet him again.'

'Yes. Does it show from my face or looks?' She asked

'Yes. You seemed to be withdrawn into yourself and have not much interest left in the outside world.'

'Yes. It can happen to anyone in my position. You will not know because you have not lost anyone dear to you.'

'But I have lost someone dear to me too. Can't you see? Look at my face.'

Sohni looked at his face and a sort of glimpse of familiarity came into her mind, similar to the one that she felt previously.

'Look at me. I am your lost love.' Karan said at least unable to sustain the mutual torture.

Sohni's head reeled by the sudden shock induced to her and she nearly fainted and was about to fall when Karan and the maid rushed forward and held her and soon Karan's arms went around her as he enclosed her in an embrace of warmth and comfort. The maid went out to let the lovers cry their hearts out. Under that emotional impact of seeing two lovers united, she was crying herself too. The lovers remained locked in their reveries, communicating with each other through their bodies, emotions, souls and through other faculties unknown to logic but felt instinctively. It looked that their feeling covered vast vistas of a being, adding something intense and profound. Love was never finished expressing itself and if the old forms of expression were obsolete, it would create new forms of its expression.

Looking from the outside and with logical eyes, it could not be comprehended by our minds but once the lovers plunged into that abyss there was no turning back from that reality of deep engendered by the mutual love. One could only say that a new poetry of emotions ushered it and those day- dreams enhanced that intensity in which the lovers lost their individual identities and fused be into some unknown.

Time was passing quickly and the maid had to come inside to separate them, dry their tears as much as she could and reminded them of their secret meeting, which might had repercussions in Sohni's household. After all she was a married woman and had to stick to moral and social codes. They had to return home before the husband noticed that his wife was missing. They need to be rational in order to avoid any such scandals.

When Sohni returned home, her mood had changed--colour had come to her cheeks and there was a spring in her walk.

In The Days of Love

She was communicating more with people around her and did extra housework for her mother in law. Even her husband noticed a change in her demeanour and was curious to find out the reason He did not want to spy on her straightway but waited to see whether her mood would change with time. No one knew about her secret rendezvous except her maid and Sohni trusted her with all her life. As a matter of fact she became her confidant and the chief instigator in arranging further meetings between the lovers. She was careful to arrange the meetings at different time and of different durations in order to keep everything secret. She watched and knew when Sohni's husband and her mother in laws were out.

The lovers took risk at meeting behind her back door or in some secret ground nearby. Sohni knew that her maid was trustworthy but in order to ensure her complete confidentiality she bribed her with extra money on top of her normal wages and often bought her new dresses. The lovers knew that they were playing a dangerous game but could not help, they wanted to make most of it while it lasted. Her husband was searching for a clue to her happiness but could not find any. He was inwardly miserable about his relations with his wife and this was an added insult as she being happy while he was miserable. This created an envy, which soon turned into jealousy and he wanted to hurt her much, to take revenge. He started spying on her and one day he returned home earlier instead of evening when he usually returned from his farm work. Luckily Sohni did not have her rendezvous on that day and so escaped being caught. He thought of other means of spying on her and about her whereabouts during the day time. He began to search for people who would do the spying for him while keeping it all a secret. He contracted some people of ill repute who were willing to do anything in exchange of a payment sufficient enough to satisfy their greed.

*

The gang of ruffians employed by the husband soon began to go around the district to find any rumours concerning his wife. They came to know that the wife in her spinster's day had too many lovers and one of those was still around and trying to entice her away from her husband. The husband was eager to hear of any such scandal, which would enable him to take a revenge on her wife, by hurting him emotionally or otherwise. He was full of bitterness and wanted any outlet for his grief however obnoxious it might be. He employed more ruffians to watch all movement of Sohni during day time and when he was out.

Soon they found a new sadhu going around the village asking for alms collecting it from various houses. Firstly they ignored him as that was the normal custom and there were bevy of such saffron coloured figures going around begging food from the householders. One of the ruffians noticed that sometime the sadhu calling on husband's house soon disappeared and could not be traced. One day they followed the sadhu when he left the village after finishing his alms round and soon found his depleted hut in a farmer's field. On the following day they broke into it when he was away and found his meager possessions but also a woman's scarf and they were happy to find some material evidence and happy that their vigils were going someplace.

One day they found Sohni and her maid in the fields surrounding the hut and soon saw them going into it. They informed the husband when he returned from his fields immediately. The husband and the gang were ready to pounce upon them as they saw them together the next time. It happened soon as they caught them 'red handed'. The husband got hold of Sohni and dragged her out of the hut pulling her by the hair all the way while the ruffian set upon Karan beating him with sticks and showering heavy blows to his body. Overwhelmed and full of rage, the husband lost his head completely.

'Kill the bastard! Kill him!' he shouted and the gang set upon Karan like mad dogs attacking a lonely animal in the fields. They were enjoying their work and giving vent to their violent nature till Karan lost all his consciousness. Then they stopped believing that he was dead and they had killed him. Meanwhile husband was dragging his wife to his house beating her all the way while a crowd gathered and followed them to the house, glad that the faithless wife got her upcomance at last. On reaching the home, the husband pushed her down the stairway to the cellar and locked the door. More and more people came to enjoy that spectacle of that cruel 'sport' in order to satisfy their lust and against that 'moral outrage.' There the poor girl lay on the dusty floor sobbing, beaten, humiliated and with torn clothes. There was no solace for her except her sobs and the cold damp air of the cellar pierced her. She had come to an end of her dignity as a human being.

She was kept locked in the damp dark cellar for a day and night and her husband had the key and would not allow anyone to unlock it. People pleaded with him to let her out but he was adamant about it. On the following day, her in laws began to get worried that she might die of beatings and hunger and forced the husband to hand over the key. Her mother in law and the maid went down to the cellar and carried her out of it and put her in a bedroom upstairs. Her condition was pitiable. Her body was dust spattered with coagulated blood all over her body and face. She was cold, hungry, shivering and sobbing. People would have pitied even an animal in that miserable condition. The maid wrapped her in a warm blanket and tried to put some hot drink into her mouth but she would not swallow and spit it out.

It happened that at that moment that their house was being decorated and walls were being painted with a sort of bluish white paint and workmen were mixing a white stuff with a compound of copper, a sort of copper of copper sulphate, neela thota, to the walls to give it a pleasant shade. Lot of this stuff was lying about in the court yard. Unknown to every one Sohni grabbed hand full of this, dissolved it in water and drank. When its affect began to take shape, the results were terrifying and horrible to watch

As the poison started to take effect, she felt that she had swallowed a beaker full of acid and all her stomach and entrails began to get entangled as if someone was squeezing them to churn all the blood out of them. Her hands and feet became icy cold and her pain unbearable and she started screaming. As people rushed in, they saw her face spattered with greenish yellow liquid, she had vomited all the contents of her stomach. She was rolling like a wounded animal and howling.

'She has poisoned herself.' Some one shouted

'Send for the doctor.'

'Oh God! Make haste. She is dying.'

The news spread quickly and all the villagers gathered around her hose. Her husband came rushing and tried to hold her but she pushed him aside defying to her last. She tried to get up from the bed but another rush of liquid issued from her mouth pushing her back. She started coughing great deal of blood.

'I am coming Karan. Wait for me.' She cried and lifted her fisted arm in defiance and then collapsed back. She was dead.

*

At the order of the husband, the ruffians took the blood soaked body of Karan to his previous dera and dumped it at its entrance. His guru was horrified and wept bitterly and nursed him to some state of health but it seemed that he had lost his mind and did not comprehend where he was and what was happening to him. The guru took him to his ancestral home to let him die in presence his family but his brothers were not pleased. He had brought so much shame on the family. He was put in a small dark room without windows and was left there with some food scattered as people feed their dogs

Somehow he managed to escape and walked all the way to where he met Sohni first time. He looked into the water and a reflection beckoned him to come forward.

'I am coming Sohni. Do not leave me alone. My love.' He cried and stepped forward into the depths of the water. The river swallowed him soon.

www.ingramcontent.com/pod-product-compliance
Lightning Source LLC
Chambersburg PA
CBHW031206270326
41931CB00006B/440